BARBARA
TAYLOR

BARNES
&NOBLE
BOOKS
NEW YORK

ISBN 0–7607–0343–4

M 10 9 8 7 6 5 4 3 2 1

© Grisewood and Dempsey Ltd. 1991, 1992

This edition published by Barnes & Noble, Inc.,
by arrangement with Larousse Kingfisher Chambers Inc.
1996 Barnes & Noble Books

The material published in this edition was previously
published by Kingfisher Books in two separate volumes
in 1991 and 1992.

Library of Congress Cataloging-in-Publication Data
available upon request.

Phototypeset by Southern Positives and Negatives
(SPAN), Lingfield, Surrey

Color separations by Scantrans pte Ltd, Singapore

Printed in Spain

CONTENTS

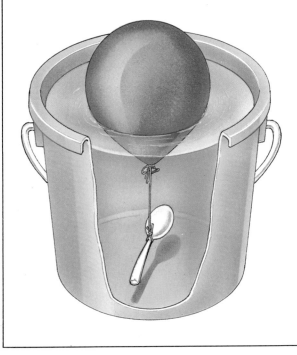

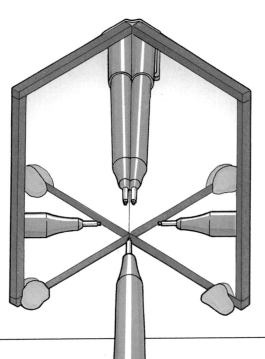

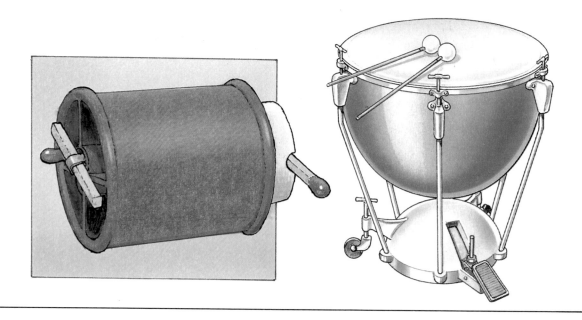

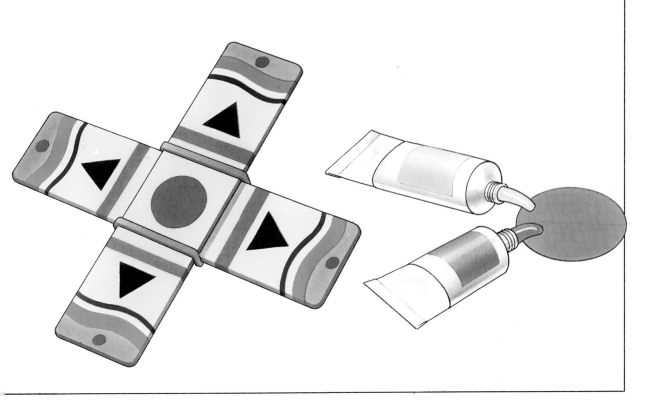

Floating and Sinking

Why do some things float and other things sink?
What shape are the fastest boats? How do submarines dive
underwater? Why do objects float higher in salty water?
What is the Plimsoll line? Why does oil float on water?
How do you make marbled paper? How deep underwater
can whales dive?

This section will help you to discover the answers to these
questions and has lots of ideas for ways to investigate
floating and sinking.

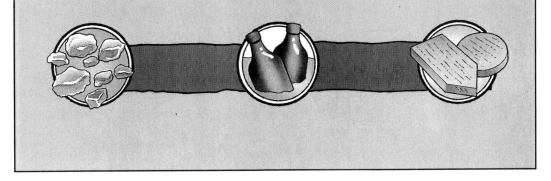

FLOATING AND SINKING

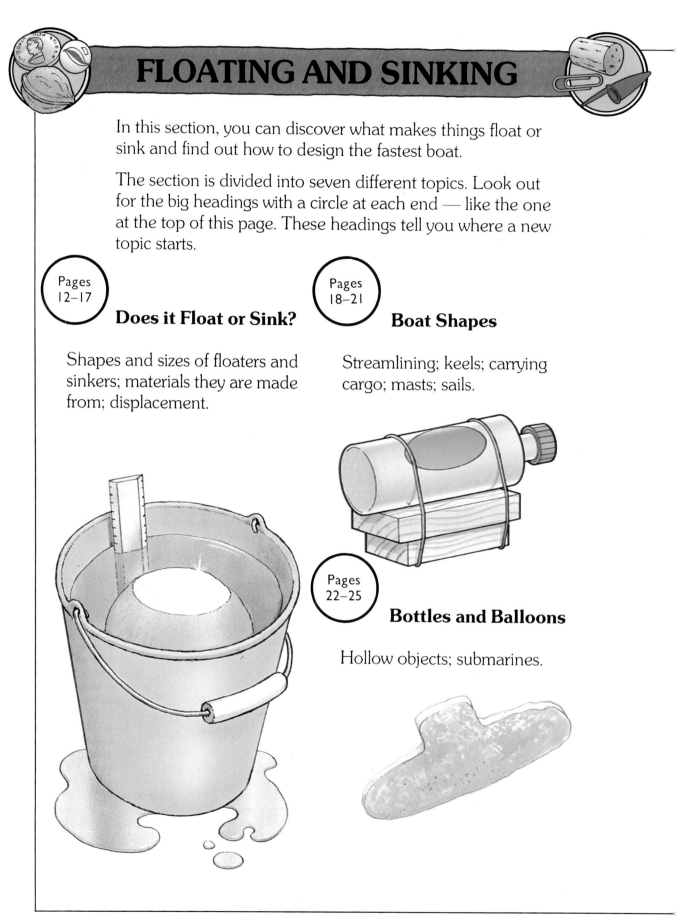

In this section, you can discover what makes things float or sink and find out how to design the fastest boat.

The section is divided into seven different topics. Look out for the big headings with a circle at each end — like the one at the top of this page. These headings tell you where a new topic starts.

Pages 12–17

Does it Float or Sink?

Shapes and sizes of floaters and sinkers; materials they are made from; displacement.

Pages 18–21

Boat Shapes

Streamlining; keels; carrying cargo; masts; sails.

Pages 22–25

Bottles and Balloons

Hollow objects; submarines.

DOES IT FLOAT OR SINK?

Look at the objects along the edges of these two pages. Which objects will float in water? Which will sink?

Make your own collection of objects to test. Choose things which are different shapes, sizes, and weights. Try to find things made from different materials, such as paper, wood, or plastic.

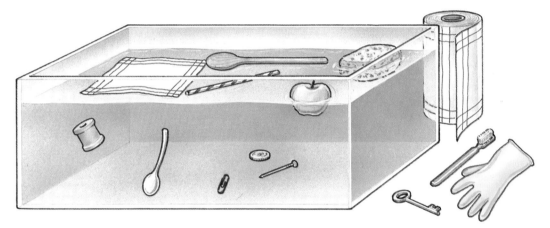

Fill a large bowl, a tank, or the bathtub with water. Put your collection of objects into the water one at a time. Before you put each object into the water, see if you can guess whether it will float or sink.

▶ Next time you are at the seashore or near a lake or a river, look carefully at any boats floating on the water. Which materials are they made from? What shape are they? You can find out more about boats on pages 12–21.

12

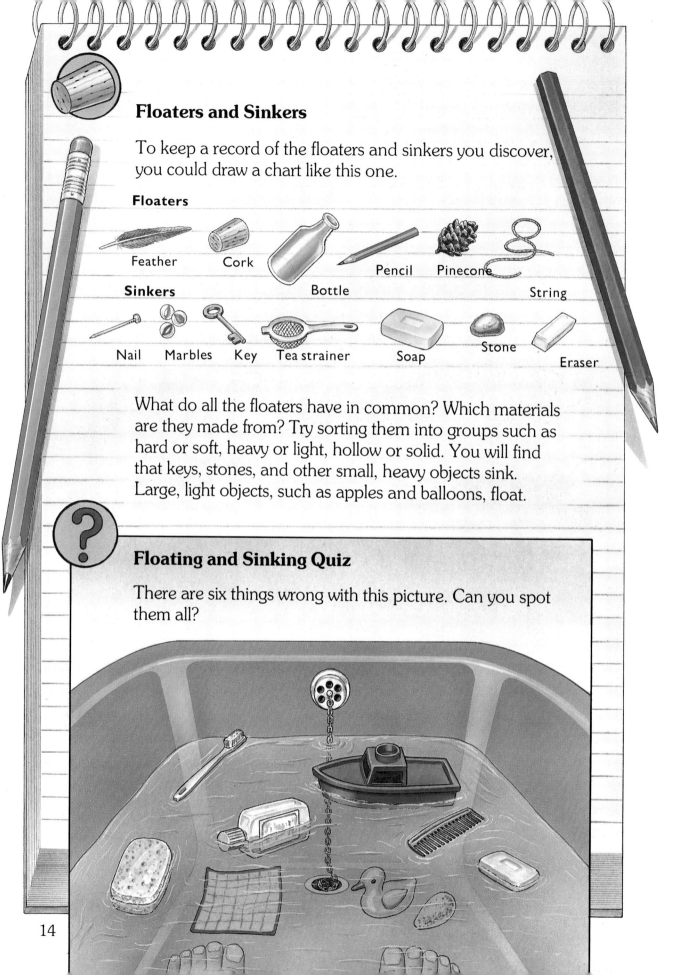

Floaters and Sinkers

To keep a record of the floaters and sinkers you discover, you could draw a chart like this one.

Floaters

Feather   Cork   Bottle   Pencil   Pinecone   String

Sinkers

Nail   Marbles   Key   Tea strainer   Soap   Stone   Eraser

What do all the floaters have in common? Which materials are they made from? Try sorting them into groups such as hard or soft, heavy or light, hollow or solid. You will find that keys, stones, and other small, heavy objects sink. Large, light objects, such as apples and balloons, float.

Floating and Sinking Quiz

There are six things wrong with this picture. Can you spot them all?

Making Floaters Sink

Did you find any objects that sometimes float and sometimes sink? For example, a paper towel floats at first but it soon soaks up the water and sinks. A limpet shell floats one way up but if you turn it over, it sinks. This photograph shows a submersible. When parts of its are filled with water, it sinks below the surface.

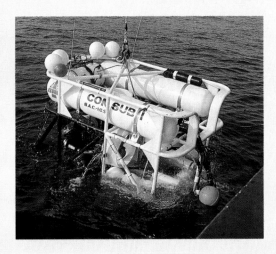

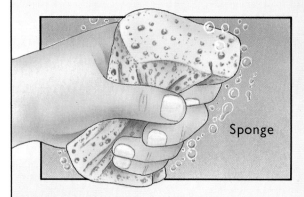

Sponge

The air holes in a sponge make it float high out of the water. Squeeze the sponge under the water. Can you see bubbles of air coming out of the sponge? When you let go of the squeezed sponge, how high does it float?

Tiny holes in the peel of a lemon contain air bubbles. The air makes the lemon float in water. But if you peel a lemon, it sinks! Try peeling an apple. Does this make the apple sink?

Lemon

Peeled lemon

Turn to page 22 to find out more about things filled with air.

Floaters

Sort your floaters into groups according to the materials they are made from. You should use groups such as wood, plastics, rubber, fabrics (wool, cotton, string, and so on).

Does All Wood Float?

Collect some different types of wood, such as oak, balsa wood, mahogany, pine, maple, and ebony. A lumberyard may let you have small pieces. Put the wood into a bowl of water. Use blocks of wood which are about the same size.

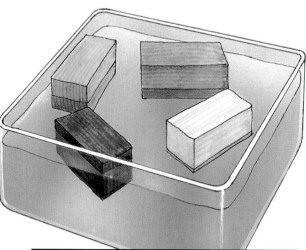

▼ In some countries, tree trunks from the forest float down a river to reach the sawmill.

What happens
You will find that the different types of wood float at different levels in the water. Balsa wood is very light and floats high out of the water. Ebony is so heavy, it sinks.

Icebergs

Huge lumps of ice floating in the sea are called icebergs. Only about a tenth of an iceberg shows above the surface of the water. This makes icebergs very dangerous to ships.

Make an Iceberg

You will need:
A balloon, water, a freezer, a ruler, scissors.

1. Fit the balloon over a cold-water faucet and fill it with water.
2. Ask an adult to help you tie the end of the balloon to seal the water inside.
3. Put the balloon inside a plastic bag (without holes) and leave the bag in a freezer overnight.
4. Next morning, take the balloon out of the freezer and, with an adult's help, use the scissors to cut away the balloon carefully.
5. Put your iceberg in a deep bucket of water. It will float, but only just. How much ice is below the water?

BOAT SHAPES

A ball of modeling clay sinks in water. But if you make the same ball of clay into a boat shape, it floats. The wide, flat boat shape pushes away more water than the narrow, round ball. The water pushes back harder against the flat shape and this holds it up on the surface of the water.

Find the Fastest Shape

Some boats, such as tugboats, are built to be strong and stable. Other boats, such as powerboats, are shaped to help them zoom through the water at high speed. This is called a streamlined shape.

Test some boat shapes yourself. Float your boats in a long piece of plastic guttering with two end pieces.

Sample shapes

With an adult's help, cut the boats out of thin balsa wood and use the same amount of wood for each boat.

Attach a weight to a long piece of thread and pin the other end of the thread to the front of each boat in turn. Measure the time each boat takes to travel the same distance. Which shape is fastest?

Gutter

Weight

 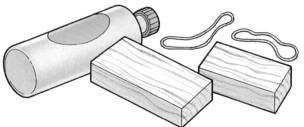

Staying Upright

Some boats have a structure called a keel on the bottom of the hull. To find out how a keel works, make one yourself.

You will need:

An empty plastic bottle, two blocks of wood (one larger than the other), thick rubber bands.

1. Put the bottle into a bowl of water and try tipping it over. You will find that it rolls over quite easily.
2. Now ask an adult to cut two blocks of wood.
3. Use the rubber bands to fix the blocks of wood under the bottle.
4. Float the bottle on the water and try tipping it over again. What happens this time?

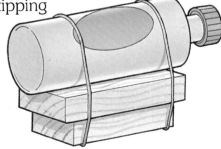

What happens

The keel keeps the weight in the center of the boat and helps it to balance in a level position on the water. It's hard to make the boat tip right over, or capsize.

▼ Keels come in all shapes and sizes. A boat with a keel cannot easily sail in shallow water.

Fooling Around with Masts

What is the best size and position for the mast on a sailing ship? To find out, cut up some plastic straws to make long, medium-length, and short masts. (Ask an adult to help you with the scissors.) Fix each mast in turn onto a balsa wood boat and try tilting the boat to one side. When you let go, does the boat tip over and capsize? Is the boat more stable with the mast in the middle of the boat or on the edge?

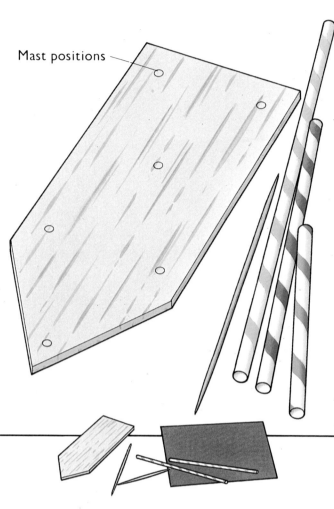

Mast positions

Super Sails

Make some sails to see how they help a boat to go faster. For the mast, use a straw, a toothpick, or a piece of thin dowel.

You could make your sails out of paper, cloth, or plastic. Blow on each sail or use a paper fan to see which sail makes the boat move fastest. What happens if you blow through a straw on just one side of a sail?

Try different shapes, sizes, and numbers of sails.

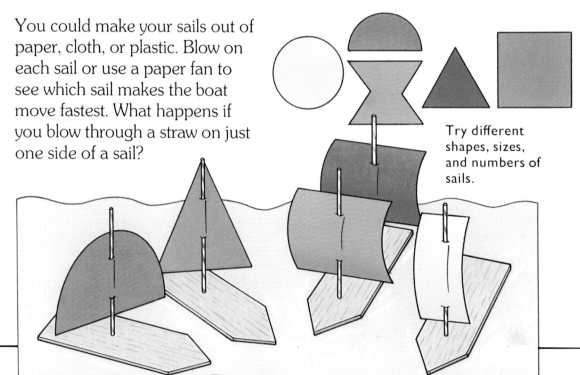

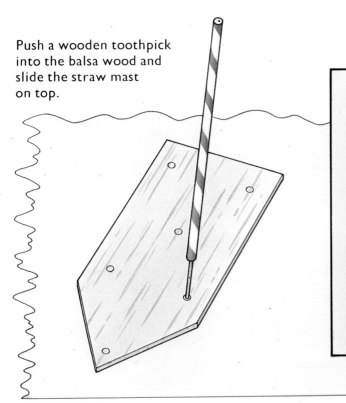

Push a wooden toothpick into the balsa wood and slide the straw mast on top.

What happens

You should find that the short mast will not make the boat capsize in any position. The medium-length mast will make the boat lean over in some positions. The long mast will make the boat capsize in some positons. Where is the best position for a long mast?

▼ How many different kinds of sail can you see on this sailing ship?

BOTTLES AND BALLOONS

Put some hollow objects into a tank or bathtub of water.
Try some of these: a plastic mug, a plastic bottle, a bowl, a pot, an empty soda can.

You will find that they all float. Can you make any of them sink?

Try pushing them under the water. Look at all the bubbles of air rising to the surface. Even though hollow things look empty, they are really full of air.

Fill a plastic bottle half full of water and put on the top. The bottle still floats in water. How much water do you have to put inside the bottle before it sinks?

Now try putting some sand inside the bottle instead of water. How much sand do you need to make the bottle sink?

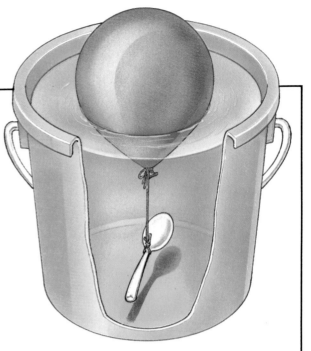

Lifting Buried Treasure

Balloons are full of air, so they float high out of the water. If you tie a balloon to a sinker, such as a metal spoon, the spoon will float underneath the balloon. Try different sinkers, such as stones, a brick, a mirror, scissors, and a screwdriver. Will the balloon lift all these sinkers off the bottom?

▼ Archeologists use special balloons to lift objects they find on an underwater dig up to the surface.

▲ Scientists such as archeologists, biologists, and engineers sometimes use small submarines to help them examine shipwrecks, living things, or man-made structures under the sea.

Make a Submarine

Submarines dive by filling tanks inside the submarine with water. They rise by pumping water out of the tanks again. If the tanks contain a lot of air, the submarine becomes lighter and rises. Make your own submarine to see how this works.

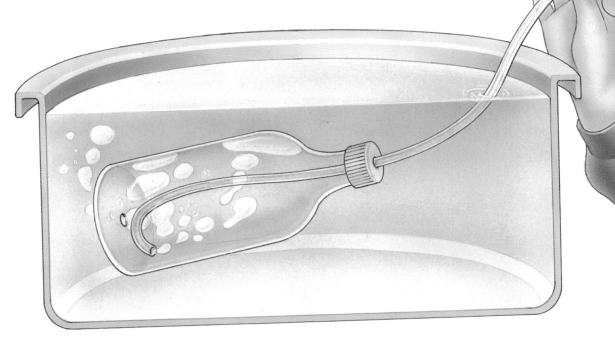

You will need:
a plastic bottle with a lid, a bowl of water, a short length of plastic tubing.

1. Ask an adult to help you make a hole in the lid of the bottle and another hole in the bottom of the bottle.
2. Ask a friend to hold her finger over the hole in the bottom of the bottle while you fill the bottle with as much water as you can.
3. Push the tubing through the hole in the bottle top and put the top on the bottle.
4. Lower the bottle carefully into the bowl of water and have your friend remove her finger from the hole. Blow hard down the plastic tube (do *not* breathe in).

What happens

As the air from your lungs goes inside the bottle, it pushes out some of the water. So the bottle rises, just like a real submarine.

25

WATER'S STRETCHY SKIN

Watch water dripping from a faucet. There is a special force on the surface of water which pulls it inward. This force is called surface tension. It gives water drops their smooth, round shape. It also makes water look as if it has a stretchy "skin" on the surface.

 Crazy Colors

Soap or liquid soap breaks down the surface tension of water and stops the skin from forming. This stops water from sticking together in drops, and so it flows more easily into all the places where dirt collects. This is one reason why water is better at cleaning things when we add soap or liquid soap.

To see what happens when water loses its skin, try this test.

Fill a shallow dish or saucer with milk and put a few drops of food coloring on top of the milk. Use a spoon to drop a small amount of liquid soap on top of the color and watch the colors explode. How long does the swirling movement last? Can you think why it stops?

Food coloring

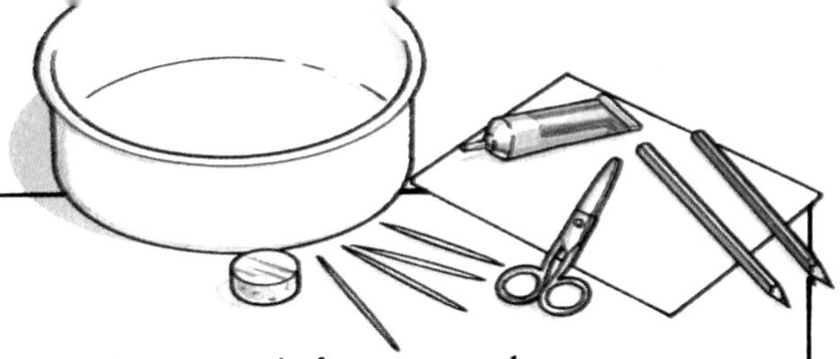

Spinning Snowman

You will need:

A bowl of water, a cork, thin balsa wood, four wooden toothpicks, mothballs, paper, scissors, glue or cellophane tape, crayons.

1. Draw and color a small snowman on the paper and cut it out.
2. Ask an adult to help you cut a slice off the cork. Cut out four small pieces of balsa wood.
3. Stick the snowman to the slice of cork.
4. Make a small notch in each of the small pieces of balsa wood and wedge a piece of mothball into each notch.
5. Stick the four toothpicks into the slice of cork to make a cross shape.
6. Fix the small pieces of balsa wood at the ends of the toothpicks.
7. Put your snowman into the bowl of water and watch it spin around.

What happens

The mothballs weaken the pull of the surface tension in the water close to them. The stronger pull of the tension in front of each mothball pulls the sticks and the snowman around in a circle. How long does the snowman keep spinning?

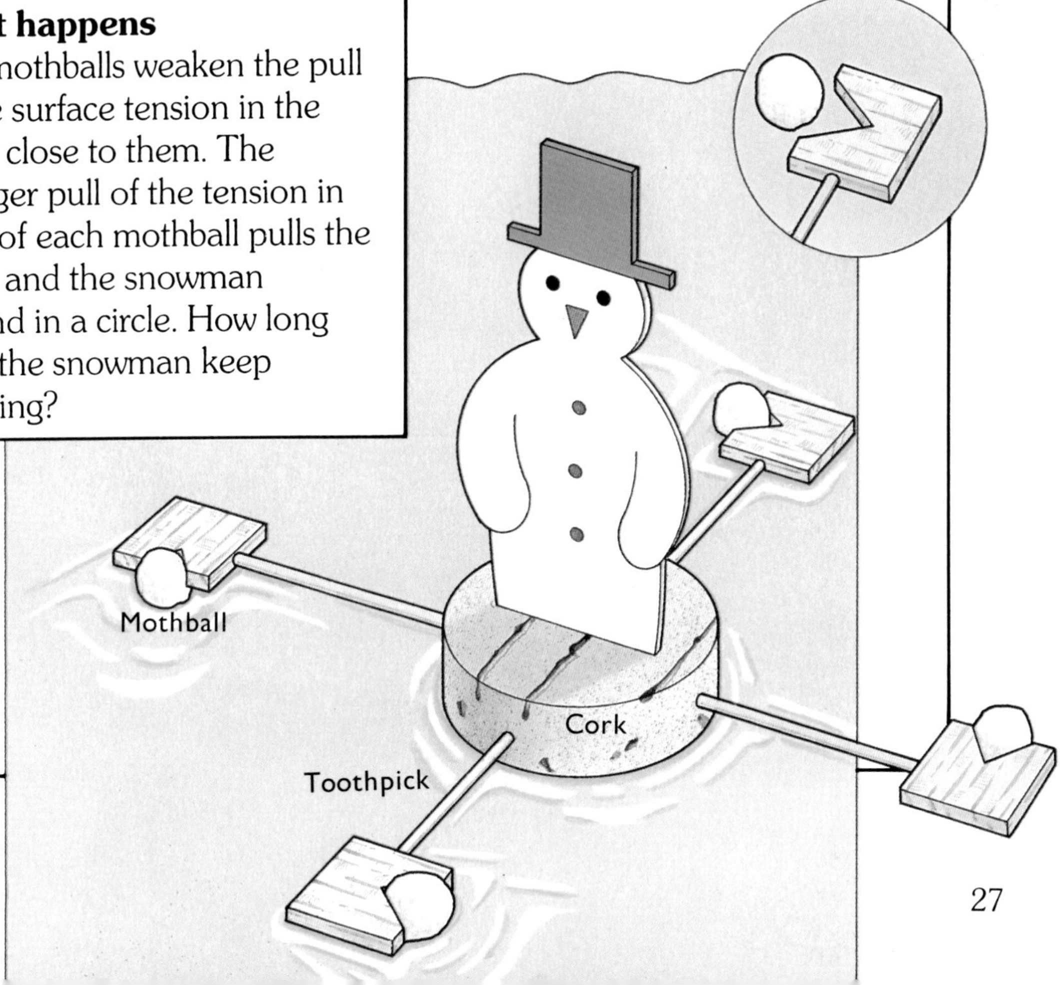

Mothball

Cork

Toothpick

27

To measure how things float in different liquids, scientists use an instrument called a hydrometer. The hydrometer sinks farther into some liquids than others. To see how it works, make one yourself.

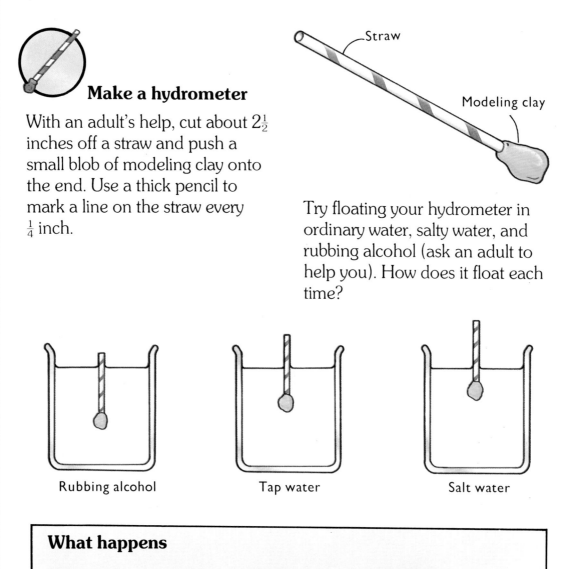

Make a hydrometer

With an adult's help, cut about $2\frac{1}{2}$ inches off a straw and push a small blob of modeling clay onto the end. Use a thick pencil to mark a line on the straw every $\frac{1}{4}$ inch.

Straw

Modeling clay

Try floating your hydrometer in ordinary water, salty water, and rubbing alcohol (ask an adult to help you). How does it float each time?

Rubbing alcohol   Tap water   Salt water

What happens

Salty water is heavier than ordinary water, so it pushes harder against objects floating in it. To float in salty water, objects need to displace less water than they do in ordinary water. So the hydrometer floats higher in salty water. In rubbing alcohol, the hydrometer floats at a lower level compared to ordinary water. This shows that rubbing alcohol is lighter than water.

Salty Surprises

An egg usually sinks in water, but this trick shows you how to make an egg look as if it floats in water. First you need to make some very salty water.

1. Fill a pan with warm tap water and add some salt.
2. Stir with a spoon and keep adding salt until you feel a gritty layer building up on the bottom of the pan.
3. Leave the salty water for several hours until it is no longer cloudy. Then it is ready to use.
4. Half fill a large jar with the salty water and put the egg into the water.
5. Now carefully pour some ordinary cold water down the side of the jar. What happens?

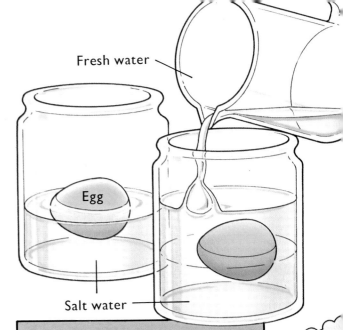

Fresh water

Egg

Salt water

What happens

The ordinary water is lighter than the salty water, so it floats on top. The egg sinks down through the ordinary water but floats on top of the salty water. It looks as if it is floating in the middle of the jar.

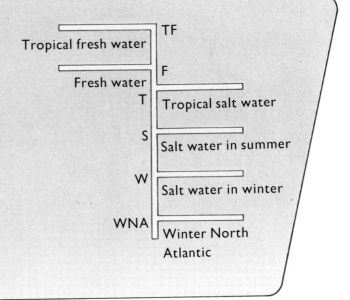

The Plimsoll Line

A ship floats at different levels depending on the weight of the cargo, the temperature of the water, and how much salt is in the water. It floats lower in fresh water than in salt water. And it floats lower in warm water than in cold water. The mark called the Plimsoll line shows the safe level for a fully loaded ship in different types of water.

Tropical fresh water — TF
Fresh water — F
T — Tropical salt water
S — Salt water in summer
W — Salt water in winter
WNA — Winter North Atlantic

Rainbow Sandwich

To find out more about how liquids float, make a rainbow sandwich.

Add food color.

Pour oil down the side of the bottle.

Rubbing alcohol and food color

Cooking oil

Water and food color

You will need:

A tall, narrow bottle (such as a soda bottle or an olive jar), cooking oil, rubbing alcohol, two different food colors.

1. Fill the bottle about a third full of water and add a few drops of one food color.
2. Carefully pour oil down the side of the bottle. It will float because oil is lighter than water.
3. Now add a layer of rubbing alcohol (ask an adult to help you). This is lighter than oil, so it floats on top of the oil. To color the top of your sandwich, add a few drops of a different food color.
4. If your bottle has a lid, you can try turning your sandwich upside down. Be careful to keep the rubbing alcohol and water apart. If they touch each other, they will mix together and you will lose half your sandwich. If this happens, start again.

▶ Workers try to collect oil which floated on top of the seawater until tides and currents washed it onto the beach.

Make a Salad Dressing

Do you know why you have to shake salad dressing before you pour it on a salad? Make some yourself to find out.

You will need:

1 tablespoon vinegar, 2 tablespoons salad oil, $\frac{1}{4}$ level teaspoon salt, some pepper, $\frac{1}{4}$ level teaspoon dry mustard, $\frac{1}{4}$ level teaspoon sugar.

1. Put the salt, pepper, mustard, and sugar into a bowl.
2. Pour on the vinegar and stir with a spoon to mix everything together.
3. Add the oil a little at a time. Each time you add more oil, beat the mixture with a fork.
4. Put the salad dressing in a bottle in the refrigerator.

5. After a while, the dressing will settle into layers. What is the top layer made of?
6. Make sure the lid is tightly on the bottle and shake it hard. What happens to the layers?

What happens

Vinegar contains water, which won't mix with the oil. The oil is lighter than the vinegar, so it floats to the top of the bottle and stays there. When you shake the dressing, the oil breaks up into little drops which hang in the vinegar for a while. This makes the dressing look cloudy. How long does the dressing take to go back into layers? If you shake the dressing longer, can you see any difference in the size of the oil drops?

The Floating Circle

This trick with floating liquids will help you understand more about why things float.

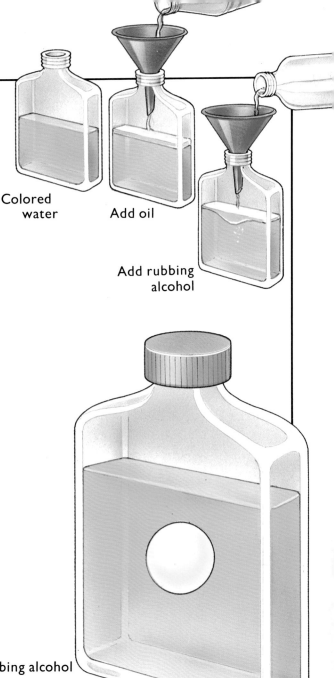

Colored water

Add oil

Add rubbing alcohol

You will need:
rubbing alcohol, cooking oil, green food coloring, water, a funnel, a small, flat bottle.

1. Fill the bottle about half full of water.
2. Add a few drops of green food coloring.
3. Use the funnel to pour a few spoonfuls of oil into the bottle.
4. Now add some rubbing alcohol (ask an adult's help) and watch how the oily layer bends in the middle.
5. Keep adding the rubbing alcohol until the oily layer becomes a circle floating in the middle of the green liquid.

After adding rubbing alcohol

What happens

When you add the rubbing alcohol, it mixes with the water and makes the water lighter (less dense). The watery mix pushes up less strongly against the oily layer, so the oil starts to sink down into the watery mix. As you add more rubbing alcohol, the watery mix starts to push on the oil equally from all directions. This makes the oil into the shape of a ball.

33

Marbling

By floating oily paints or inks on the surface of water, you can make wonderful swirly patterns to decorate paper. This is called marbling because the patterns are like the ones you can see in pieces of polished marble.

You will need:

An old bowl, marbling inks or oil paints, plain paper, a straw or old fork, newspaper. (If you don't have any oil paints, use some powder paint mixed with cooking oil.)

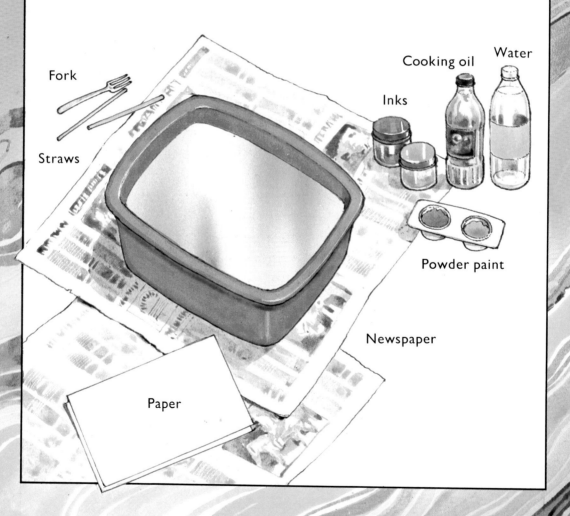

Fork

Straws

Inks

Cooking oil

Water

Powder paint

Newspaper

Paper

1. Put plenty of newspaper on the floor and put on an apron.
2. Put the bowl in the middle of the newspaper and fill it half full of water.
3. Drop two or three different colors onto the water in turn. You don't need much of each color.
4. Use the straw or the fork to swirl the paint carefully around until you make a pattern that you like.
5. Now gently lay a piece of thick paper flat on the surface of the water and quickly lift it off again.
6. Hold the paper over the bowl until most of the water has dripped off into the bowl.
7. Let the paper dry.
8. When the paper is dry, you can use it to wrap presents or cover books and pencils.

Hint: To clear the water of old colors, put a paper towel on the surface of the water. It will soak up the colors so you can lift them out of the water.

SINKING TO THE BOTTOM

Rocks such as sandstone are formed from layers of sandy particles which settle one on top of another. This often happens underwater when sandy particles washed off the land near a river sink down to the bottom of an ocean or lake. As more and more sand collects, the weight presses the layers together and squeezes the water out. Over millions of years, the sand becomes hard enough to form rocks.

You can experiment with soil particles to find out more about how rocks form.

Find a large jar with a lid and put in some garden soil until the jar is about one-third full. Fill the rest of the jar with water. Put on the lid, shake the jar, and let it settle. After a few days, you should be able to see different layers in the jar.

Each layer is made up of particles of a different size. Are the biggest particles on the top or the bottom?

Cleaning Water

The way small particles sink down through water is used to help us clean the water we drink. At the waterworks, the dirty water from rivers and wells goes through big tanks where all the tiny pieces sink to the bottom and are taken out. Then the water goes through filters made of sand and gravel. These trap other dirt which sinks down through the water and into the sand.

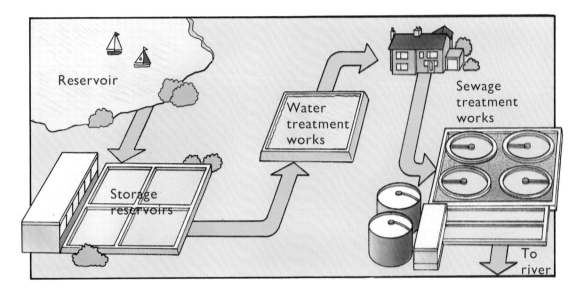

These are filter beds where the dirt is trapped.

Marlin

Water wings full of air help us to float.

Marlin can reach speeds of up to 50 miles per hour. Their streamlined shape helps them to move quickly through the water.

Divers wear a weight belt so they can rise and sink.

The sperm whale can dive to about 10,000 feet to search for food. But it has to come to the surface to breathe air after an hour or so.

This seaweed has air bladders to help it to float.

Bladder wrack

Sperm whale

Flat duckweed leaves float on the surface.

Pondweed flowers float on the surface but the leaves stay underwater.

Water crowfoot

Water crowfoot has flat, glossy floating leaves and fernlike underwater leaves. The underwater leaves bend easily when the water moves.

Floating Green Stuff

Plants that float on or in water have special shapes and structures to help them survive. Most water plants have lots of air spaces inside them to keep them upright and floating in the water.

You can make your own underwater garden in a large tank or jar. Buy or take cuttings of plants such as duckweed, water lily, eelgrass, and arrowhead.

TRUE OR FALSE?

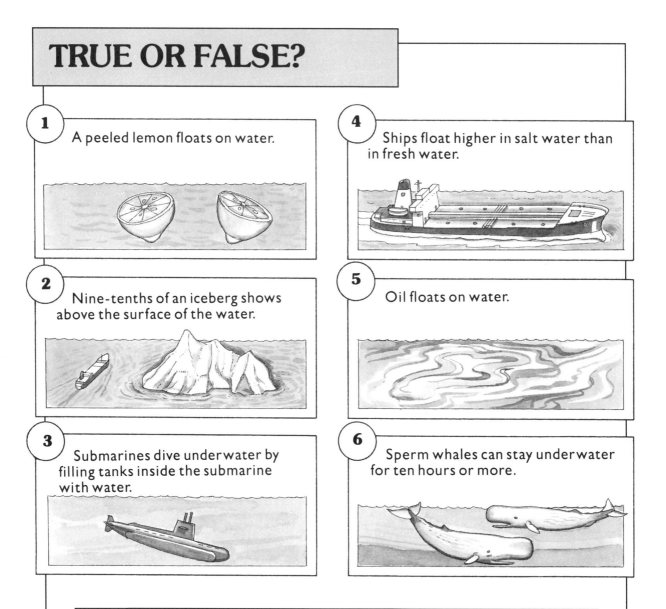

1 A peeled lemon floats on water.

2 Nine-tenths of an iceberg shows above the surface of the water.

3 Submarines dive underwater by filling tanks inside the submarine with water.

4 Ships float higher in salt water than in fresh water.

5 Oil floats on water.

6 Sperm whales can stay underwater for ten hours or more.

Shadows and Reflections

Why do shadows form? How can you make animal shadows? How does the size of shadows change at different times of day? How does a sundial use shadows to tell the time? What is an eclipse? Which materials give the best reflections? How does a periscope work?

This section will help you to discover the answers to these questions and has lots of ideas for ways to investigate shadows and reflections.

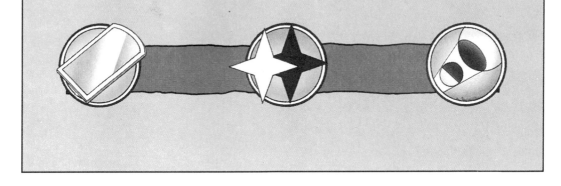

SHADOWS AND REFLECTIONS

In this section, you can discover how and why shadows form and take a closer look at the reflections in mirrors and other shiny materials.

The section is divided into five different topics. Look out for the big headings with a circle at each end — like the one at the top of this page. These headings tell you where a new topic starts.

(Pages 44–49) **Light and Shadows**

Transparent, translucent, and opaque materials; how light travels; shadow shapes.

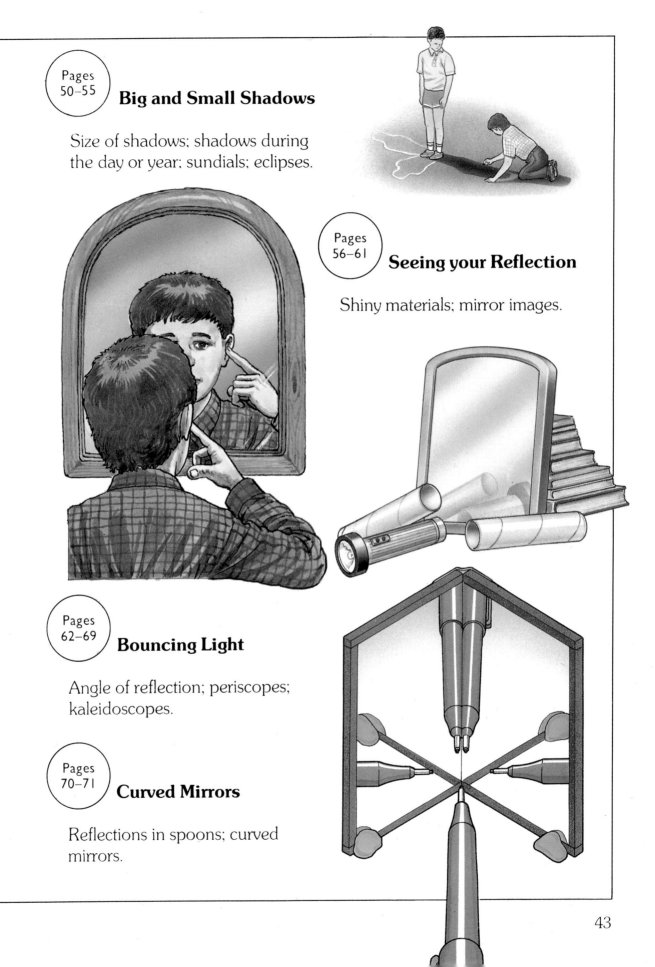

LIGHT AND SHADOWS

Make a collection of objects like the ones along the edges of these two pages. In a dark room, shine a torch onto each object. Which objects let the light through? Which objects keep out the light?

Some things let light go straight through them. You can see clearly through these things. They are said to be transparent. Clear glass and clean water are transparent.

Some things let light through but they scatter the light. If you look through these materials, everything looks blurred. These materials are said to be translucent. Frosted glass and tracing paper are translucent.

Many things do not let any light pass through them. You cannot see through these things. They are said to be opaque. Your body is opaque, so is this book.

In this picture can you find a transparent material, a translucent material, and an opaque material?

45

Going Straight

When light hits an opaque object, a dark area forms behind the object. This is called a shadow. Why doesn't light bend round objects and light up the shadow area? To find out, try this test.

1. Cut two pieces of cardboard about 8 inches square.
2. To find the middle of the cardboard, draw a line from each corner to the opposite corner. The point where the lines cross is the middle of the cardboard.
3. Cut a hole in the middle of each piece of cardboard.
4. Use modeling clay to fix the

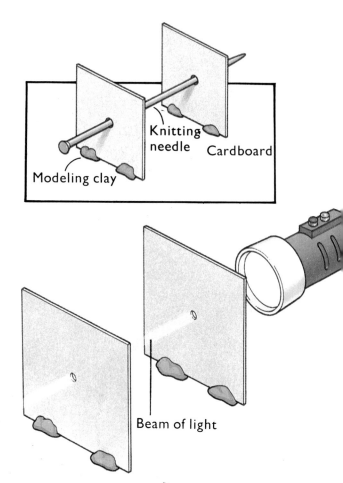

Knitting needle · Cardboard · Modeling clay

Beam of light

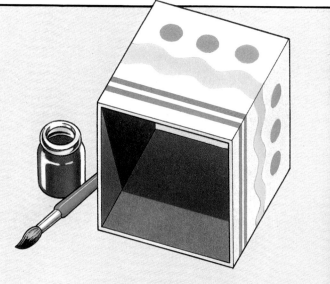

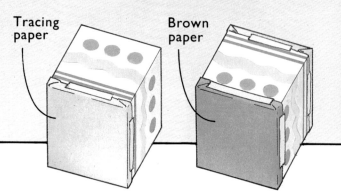

Make a Pinhole Camera

To investigate how light travels, try making a pinhole camera.

You will need:

An empty box, thick brown paper, tracing paper, a pin, scissors, sticky tape, black paint, charcoal or a thick black felt pen, a dark cloth or towel.

1. Cut both ends off the box.
2. Paint or color the inside of the box black.
3. Tape a piece of brown paper over one end of the box.

Tracing paper   Brown paper

cards upright about 12 inches apart. To line up the holes in a straight line, push a knitting needle through both holes.

5. Ask a friend to shine a light on to the first hole. You should see the light go through the second hole.

6. Now move the second card to one side so the holes are not in a straight line. What happens?

What happens
Light travels in straight lines and cannot bend around things. So when you move the second card out of line, the light cannot get through the second hole.

▲ Can you see the straight edges of these beams of sunlight?

4. Tape a piece of tracing paper over the other end.

5. Use the pin to make a small, round hole in the middle of the brown paper.

6. Cover your head and the tracing paper end of the box with the cloth or towel.

7. Point the camera at a window and look at the tracing paper from about 6 inches away. You should see an upside-down window.

What happens
Light from the top of the window passes in a straight line through

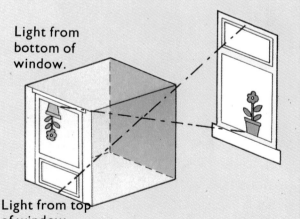

Light from bottom of window.

Light from top of window.

the pinhole to the bottom of the tracing paper. Light from the bottom of the window travels to the top of the tracing paper. So the picture you see is upside-down.

Shadow Shapes

Find lots of small objects and see how many different shadow shapes you can make.

A shadow is the same shape as the outside edge of an object. To change the shape of a shadow, move the object around or move the position of the light.

Make a shadow of an object with a hole in the middle. In the shadow, can you make the hole disappear? Try making shadows on different surfaces, such as wood, grass, or the stairs. How do the shadows change?

Ask a friend to look only at the shadows of some objects and guess what the objects are. Turn the objects so that the shadows are hard to recognize.

Shadow Portraits

1. Ask a friend to sit sideways on a chair near a wall.
2. Use masking tape to fix a sheet of paper to the wall behind your friend's head.
3. Shine a torch so your friend's head casts a shadow on the paper.
4. Draw around the edge of the shadow with the pencil.
5. Paint inside the outline.

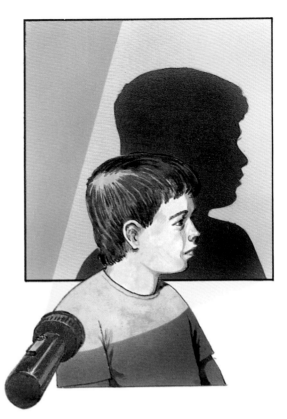

Animal Shadows

With your hands, you can make animal shadows. Here are some ideas. How many more can you discover?

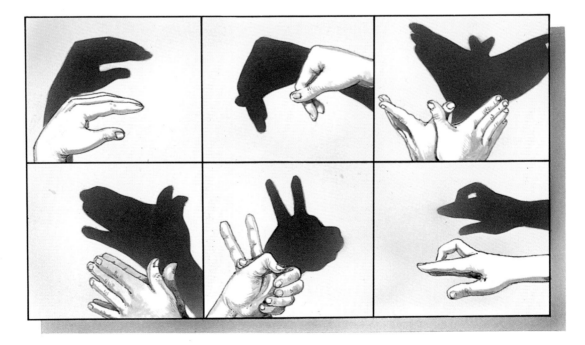

BIG AND SMALL SHADOWS

Cut out a star shape from a piece of cardboard and fix it to a pencil with modeling clay. Prop up a large piece of white paper on some books. In a dark room, shine a flashlight onto your star.

Hold the star near the flashlight.
How big is the shadow?

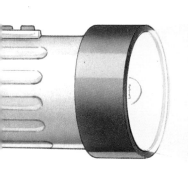

Now move the star farther away from the flashlight.
What happens to the shadow. Is it bigger or smaller?
What happens to the size of the shadow if you keep the star in one place and move the flashlight backward and forward?

What happens
When the star is near the light, it blocks out a lot of light, so the shadow is big. When the star is farther away from the light, it blocks out less light, so the shadow is smaller.

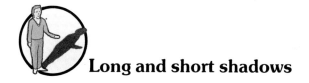

Long and short shadows

On a sunny day, find a safe area of concrete or asphalt—not out in the street. Ask if you can use chalk to draw around shadows. With a friend, stand in the same place in the early morning, at midday, and in late afternoon. Take turns standing still while one of you draws around the other's shadow.

Measure your shadows from head to toe. How does the size of the shadows change at different times of the day? Which direction do your shadows point at different times of the day—north, south, east, or west?

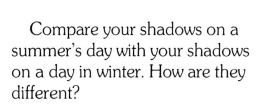

Compare your shadows on a summer's day with your shadows on a day in winter. How are they different?

What happens
In the early morning or late afternoon, the Sun is low in the sky and shadows are long. At midday, the Sun is high above you and your shadows are shorter. In winter, the Sun is lower in the sky than it is in summer. So winter shadows are longer than summer shadows.

You will need: a pencil or a short stick, a thread spool, glue or modeling clay, a large piece of white paper.

Make a Shadow Clock

You can use shadows to help you tell the time. Here's how to make a shadow clock.

1. Stand a pencil or a short stick in a thread spool.
2. Use glue or modeling clay to fix the spool to a large piece of white paper.
3. On a sunny day, put your shadow clock out of doors where the Sun will shine on it.
4. Draw a line along the shadow of the stick and write the time at the end of the line.
5. Do the same thing every hour.

12 o'clock

11 o'clock

10 o'clock

9 o'clock

8 o'clock

7 o'clock

◀ A sundial is a type of shadow clock which was invented more than 3,000 years ago, long before watches were made.

Shadows in Space

The Moon has no light of its own. It shines because it reflects light from the Sun. Sometimes, the Earth moves in a direct line between the Moon and the Sun and stops Sunlight from reaching the Moon. The Earth's shadow makes the Moon look very dark for a while. This is called a lunar eclipse. "Lunar" means to do with the Moon.

Try this investigation to see how a lunar eclipse works.

Use a large beachball or a soccer ball as the Earth and a small table tennis ball as the Moon. Stick a piece of string to the "Moon" so you can hang it in front of the "Earth." Use a flashlight or a table lamp as the Sun.

Shadow

Small ball

Large ball

Can you make the "Earth" cast a shadow on the "Moon?" What happens to the shadow if you move the "Moon" in a circle around the "Earth?"

▲ This photograph shows what happens when the Moon passes in front of the Sun. It stops sunlight from reaching the Earth and makes some places on Earth dark during the daytime. This is called a solar eclipse—"solar" means to do with the Sun.

For a solar eclipse to happen, the Moon, the Sun and the Earth all have to be in a straight line. This does not happen very often.

Reflections and Materials

How many things can you find in which you can *see* your reflection? Look for your reflection out of doors in store windows, car hoods, and buildings. Can you *see* your reflection in water? What happens to your reflection if the water is moving?

In a dark room, shine a flashlight onto different materials such as aluminum foil, brick, wood, plastic, cloth, and metal. Which materials give the best reflections?

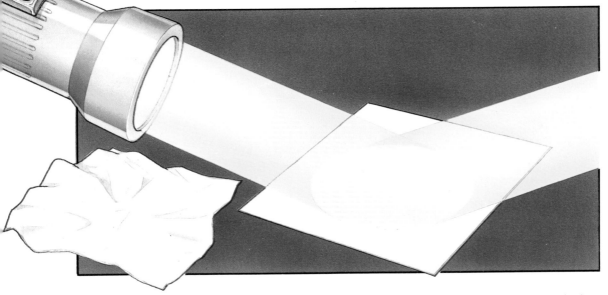

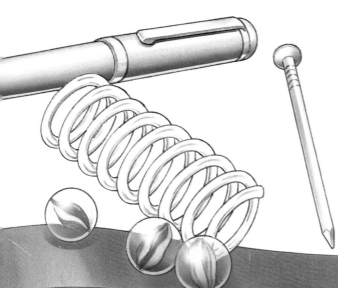

Compare a smooth piece of foil with a wrinkled piece of foil. Can you *see* your face in both pieces of foil?

Make a collection of shiny materials. You could sort your collection into groups according to the materials the objects are made of—metal or non-metal for example.

Mirror, Mirror

Smooth, shiny surfaces produce the best reflections. This is why mirrors are made of a flat sheet of glass with a thin layer of shiny metal, such as silver or aluminum behind the glass.

To make your own mirror, glue a piece of aluminum foil to a piece of thin cardboard. Make sure the foil is smooth and has no wrinkles. What can you see in your mirror? Is it as good as a real mirror? How are the reflections different?

How many different mirrors can you find at home, at school, along the street or in the stores? What shapes and sizes are they? How are they used?

▶ Dancers and actors would find it difficult to put on their makeup properly without a mirror.

Matching Quiz

Some things can be divided by an imaginary line into two parts that look exactly the same. These things are called symmetrical objects. You can find out if something is symmetrical by putting a mirror along the dividing line. If the object looks the same in the mirror, it has a kind of symmetry.

See if you can guess which of the objects below are symmetrical. Test them by holding a mirror against each picture.

Leaf

Orange

Flashlight

Scissors

Snowflake

Shell

Glove

Feather

Key

Tennis racket

Cup

Funny Faces

Is your face symmetrical? Find a photograph of yourself which shows your whole face from the front. Hold a mirror down the middle of the photograph. Look at both sides of your face. Does your face look strange?

Mirror Painting

To make a symmetrical painting, you will need: newspaper, plain paper, poster paints, jar of water, paintbrush, apron.

1. Put on the apron and lay some newspaper on a table or on the floor so you won't make a mess.
2. Mix up several different colors with the poster paints. Make each color fairly thick.
3. Use the brush to drop or brush paint onto one side of the paper.
4. Fold the paper over and press down to smooth out the paint.

What happens

When you open out the paper, you will have a painting that is the same on both sides, just as if you were looking in a mirror.

BOUNCING LIGHT

Reflections are caused by light bouncing off things. When this light is reflected into our eyes, we are able to see things.

Catch the Light

Use a small mirror to reflect a spot of light from the Sun or a lamp onto a wall. If you turn the mirror a little, the light spot will move too. Ask a friend to make another light spot on the same wall. Can your friend touch your light spot with the one they have made?

Bouncing Back

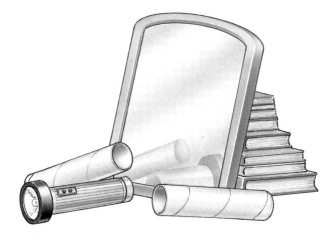

When light hits a smooth surface, it always bounces back at a matching angle. To see how this works, try this test.

You will need: a large mirror, two cardboard tubes, a flashlight, some books.

1. Use the books to prop the mirror upright.
2. Hold one tube at an angle with the end touching the mirror.
3. Ask a friend to hold the second tube at a matching angle.

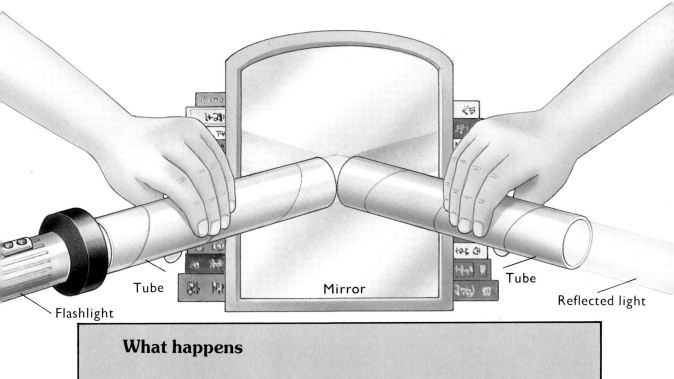

Flashlight

Tube

Mirror

Tube

Reflected light

What happens

When the tubes are at the correct angle, the light will bounce off the mirror and down to the end of the second tube. If your friend holds his or her hand at the end of the tube, they will see a circle of reflected light.

On a rough surface, light is not reflected like this. It is scattered back in several different directions.

Multiplying Mirrors

When two mirrors are held together at an angle, the light bounces to and fro between the mirrors. This means you can see more than one reflection of an object.

Tape two mirrors together along one of the long sides. Use some modeling clay to stand the mirrors upright at a wide angle. Put a small object in front of the mirrors. How many reflections can you see?

Now move the mirrors closer together. Count how many reflections of the object you can see now.

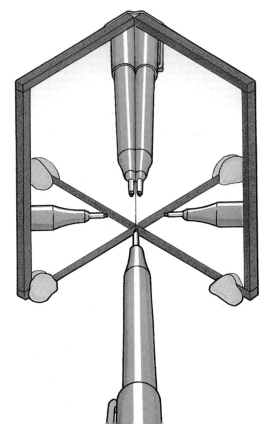

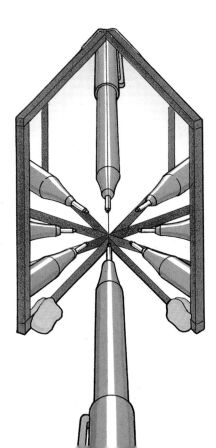

Your Other Face

You can use two mirrors to see yourself as other people see you. To see how this works, you need to make one side of your face look different from the other side. You could use face paints to do this.

Look in one mirror and remember where the painted side of your face appears on your reflection. Then hold two mirrors facing each other at an angle. Move the mirrors until you can see your whole face at the point where the two mirrors join. The painted side of your face will now be on the other side of your reflection.

What happens

With the mirrors at an angle, the reflection of the left side of your face bounces across to the right hand mirror. And the reflection of the right side of your face bounces across to the left hand mirror. When other people look straight at you, they see your face this way around.

How Many Reflections?

Hold a small mirror facing a large mirror so the small mirror is just in front of your nose. As you look over the top of the small mirror, you will be able to see lots and lots of reflections stretching away into the distance. How many reflections can you see? Are all the reflections the same size?

 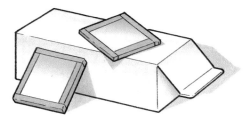

Make a Periscope

Have you ever had your view blocked by a crowd of people? By making a periscope you will be able to see over their heads so you won't miss anything. You can also use a periscope to look around a corner or over a wall without being seen.

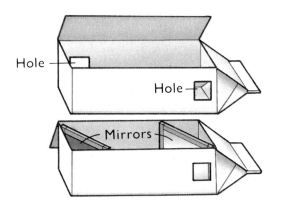

Hole

Hole

Mirrors

You will need: a large empty milk or juice carton, two small mirrors, sticky tape, scissors.

1. On one side of the carton, cut three of the edges to make a lid you can lift up.
2. Cut two holes in opposite sides of the carton, to match the picture.
3. Tape the two mirrors inside the carton. The mirrors should be facing each other at the same angle.
4. Tape down the lid.
5. Hold the periscope upright and look into the bottom mirror.

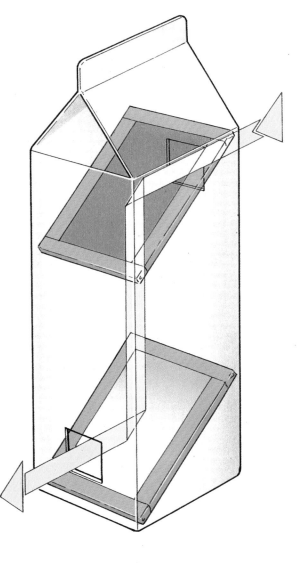

What happens

The light bounces from one mirror to the other so you can see over people's heads or around corners.

Using periscopes, even people at the back of a large crowd can see what is happening at the front.

Make a Kaleidoscope

The word "kaleidoscope" means "beautiful to look at." If you make a kaleidoscope, you will be able to see lots of beautiful symmetrical patterns.

You will need: stiff cardboard, a pencil, scissors, black paper or a thick black felt pen, aluminum foil, glue, clear plastic, tracing paper, sticky tape, small colored shapes or beads.

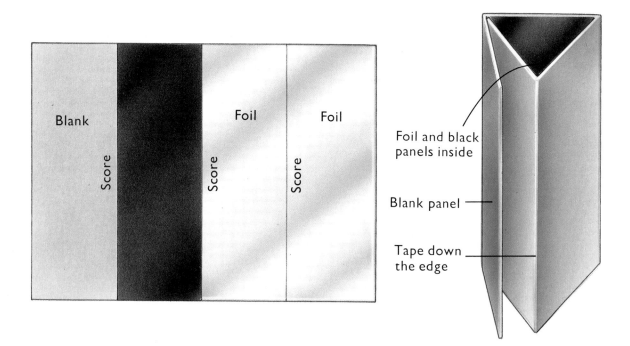

1. Cut out a piece of cardboard about 9 inches by 6 inches.
2. With the pencil, divide the card into four equal strips. Each strip should be $1\frac{1}{2}$ inches wide.
3. Ask an adult to help you score the lines so the cardboard is easier to fold.

4. Stick foil over two of the panels. Make sure it is as smooth as possible.
5. Stick black paper over the third panel or color it black.
6. Leave the fourth panel blank.
7. Fold the cardboard to make a triangular shape and tape the side to hold it in place.

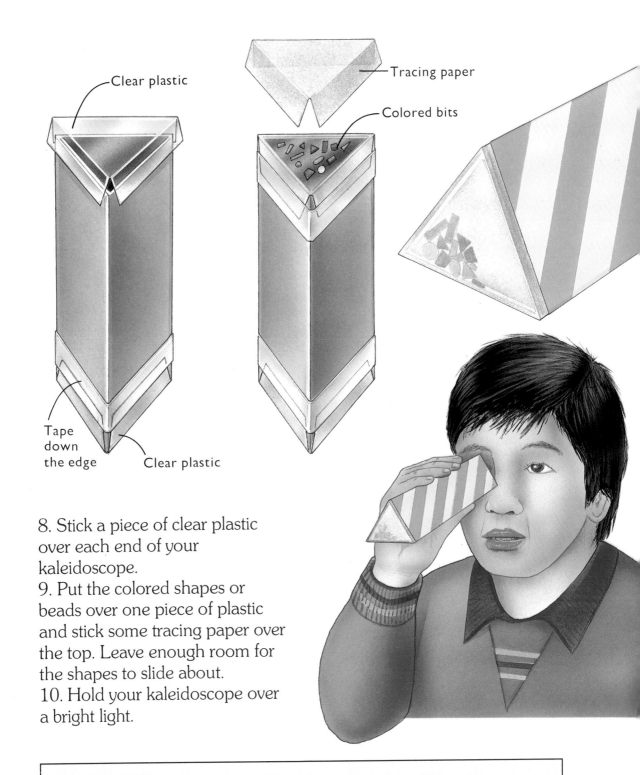

Clear plastic

Tracing paper

Colored bits

Tape
down
the edge

Clear plastic

8. Stick a piece of clear plastic over each end of your kaleidoscope.

9. Put the colored shapes or beads over one piece of plastic and stick some tracing paper over the top. Leave enough room for the shapes to slide about.

10. Hold your kaleidoscope over a bright light.

What happens
The light bounces to and fro between the foil mirrors. The reflections of the colored shapes or beads make interesting patterns. To change the pattern, shake your kaleidoscope so the shapes or beads move into new positions.

CURVED MIRRORS

Curved mirrors change the size and shape of things reflected in them. Look at your reflection in the curved side of a shiny tin or a pot. What do you look like?

Now try a spoon. The back of a spoon curves outward. This sort of curved mirror makes you look smaller.

What happens to your reflection in the front of a spoon?

▶ The surfaces of these curved mirrors curve both inward and outward. Look what it does to these reflections!

TRUE OR FALSE?

1 This book is opaque.

2 If an object is near to a source of light, it casts a small shadow.

3 Winter shadows are shorter than summer shadows.

4 The Moon does not produce any light of its own.

5 In the front of a spoon, a reflection looks upside down.

6 You can use a periscope to see through a wall.

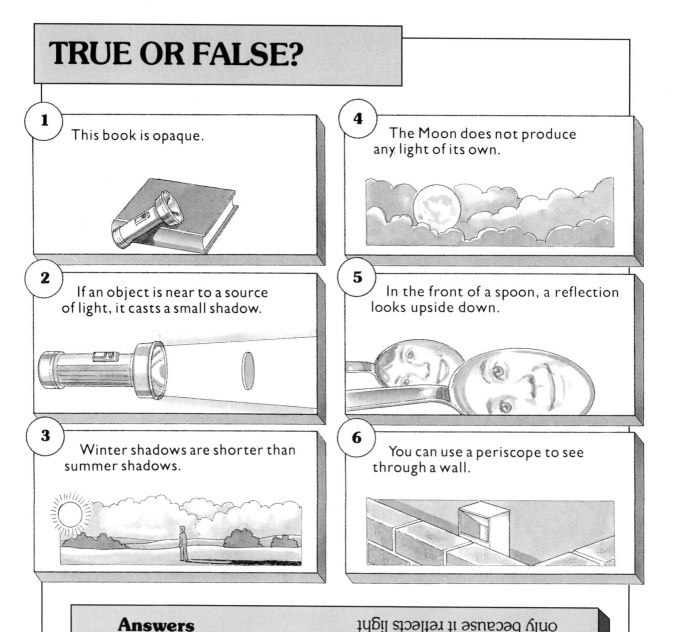

Answers

1 True. You cannot see through the book because it does not allow light to pass through it.

2 False. The object blocks out a lot of light and casts a big shadow.

3 False. In winter, the Sun is low in the sky, so shadows are longer than in summer.

4 True. The Moon shines only because it reflects light from the Sun.

5 True. The way the light is reflected from the curved surface makes the reflection appear upside down.

6 False. Periscopes allow you to see over the top of a wall or round a corner, but not through solid materials.

Machines and Movement

How is your arm like a lever? How does a gymnast keep her balance on a beam? How is a mobile like a see-saw? How do pulleys help us to lift heavy weights? What do gear wheels do? How do forces called friction and gravity affect movement on Earth and in space? How can you use a rubber band to make a weighing machine?

This section will help you to discover the answers to these questions and has lots of ideas for ways to investigate machines and movement.

MACHINES AND MOVEMENT

In this section. you can discover how machines make our lives easier and how forces such as friction and gravity affect movement.

The section is divided into eight different topics. Look out for the big headings with a circle at each end — like the one at the top of this page. These headings tell you where a new topic starts.

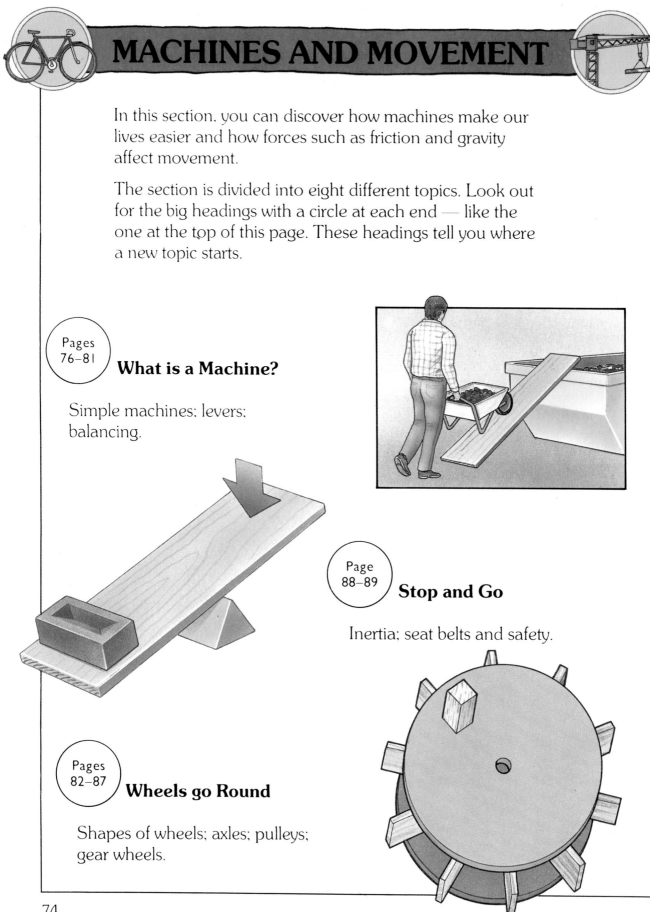

Pages 76–81

What is a Machine?

Simple machines: levers: balancing.

Page 88–89

Stop and Go

Inertia; seat belts and safety.

Pages 82–87

Wheels go Round

Shapes of wheels; axles; pulleys; gear wheels.

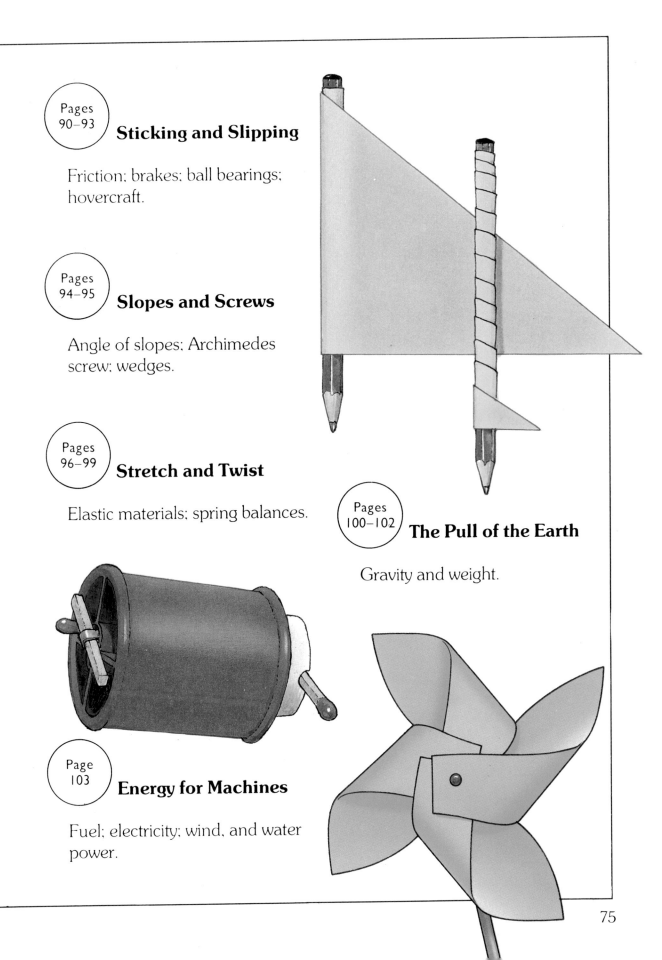

WHAT IS A MACHINE?

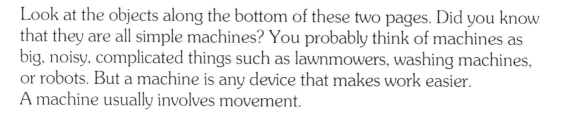

Look at the objects along the bottom of these two pages. Did you know that they are all simple machines? You probably think of machines as big, noisy, complicated things such as lawnmowers, washing machines, or robots. But a machine is any device that makes work easier. A machine usually involves movement.

Scissors make it easier to cut things.
A bicycle makes it easier to go fast.
A screw helps to hold pieces of wood together.
A spade makes it easier to dig the garden.
A crane makes it easier to lift heavy weights.

Lever

Wheel

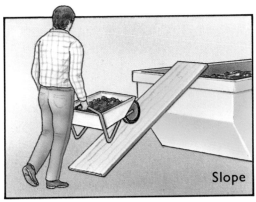

Slope

Wedge

There are five very simple machines that are the basis of all the other machines we use. They are:

the lever
the wheel
the slope
the screw
the wedge

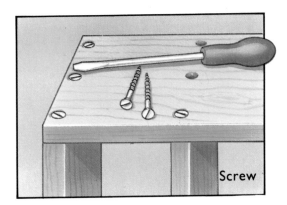

Screw

Look out for these machines as you read this book. Try making a list of all the machines in your home or school. Which room has the most machines?

Lifting with Levers

A lever is a bar that pivots on a fixed point called a fulcrum. A lever makes it easier to lift heavy things. Your arm is a kind of lever. So are scissors, spades, pliers, tweezers, brooms, wheelbarrows, and seesaws. If you push one end of a lever down, the other end moves up.

Make a lever by balancing a plank of wood over a small block of wood. The block is the fulcrum. Try lifting a brick with your lever. Is it easier to lift the brick if the fulcrum is nearer to the brick or farther away?

Effort

Load

Fulcrum

There are three kinds of lever. Each one has the pushing force (the effort), the pivot (fulcrum), and the weight (the load) in different places. This allows each of them to do a different job.

1st class lever

Effort

Load

Fulcrum

2nd class lever

Effort

Fulcrum   Load

3rd class lever

Fulcrum

Effort

Load

A first class lever has the fulcrum between the effort and the load.
A second class lever has the load between the effort and the fulcrum.
A third class lever has the effort between the fulcrum and the load.

▲ In this picture, the tennis player's arm is working as a third class lever. The effort is the muscles of the upper arm, which are in between the fulcrum (the shoulder) and the load (the ball hitting the racket).

Balancing

How good are you at balancing?
Put a ball on the floor near a wall.
Stand with your heels right up
against the wall. Now try to pick
up the ball without moving your
feet.

It's impossible! When you bend over, your balancing point moves
foward. To keep your balance, you have to move your feet forward too.
The balancing point of an object is called its center of gravity .

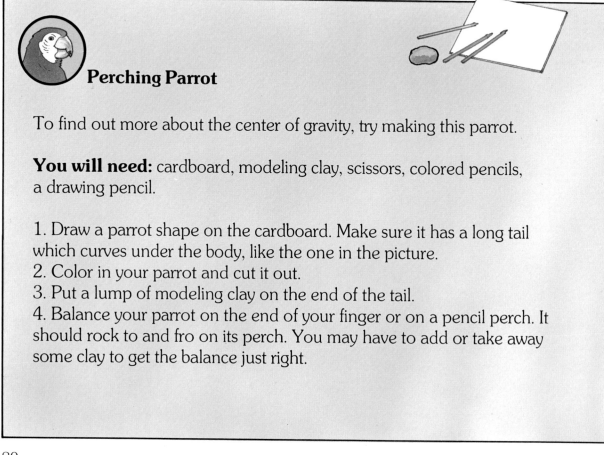

Perching Parrot

To find out more about the center of gravity, try making this parrot.

You will need: cardboard, modeling clay, scissors, colored pencils,
a drawing pencil.

1. Draw a parrot shape on the cardboard. Make sure it has a long tail
which curves under the body, like the one in the picture.
2. Color in your parrot and cut it out.
3. Put a lump of modeling clay on the end of the tail.
4. Balance your parrot on the end of your finger or on a pencil perch. It
should rock to and fro on its perch. You may have to add or take away
some clay to get the balance just right.

▲ On the balance beam, a gymnast has to keep her center of gravity right in the middle of her body. Otherwise she will fall off the beam.

Modeling clay

What happens
The weight of modeling clay makes the center of gravity of the parrot occur just below the point where it touches the perch. This makes the parrot balance. What happens if you take away some of the modeling clay?

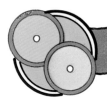

WHEELS GO AROUND

Wheels help us to move things along the ground. They are also used to make pots and spin wool. What else are wheels used for?

Wheels and Axles

A wheel on its own is not much use. It needs something to turn on. This is called an axle. Use straws, pencils, or thin dowel as axles and cut out wheels from thin cardboard or balsa wood. Use modeling clay to fix the axles to the wheels. You can make the axle and the wheel turn together. Or you can leave the wheel free to turn while the axle stays still.

What happens if the axle is not in the middle of the wheel? Try making different shaped wheels. Which shape turns around most easily?

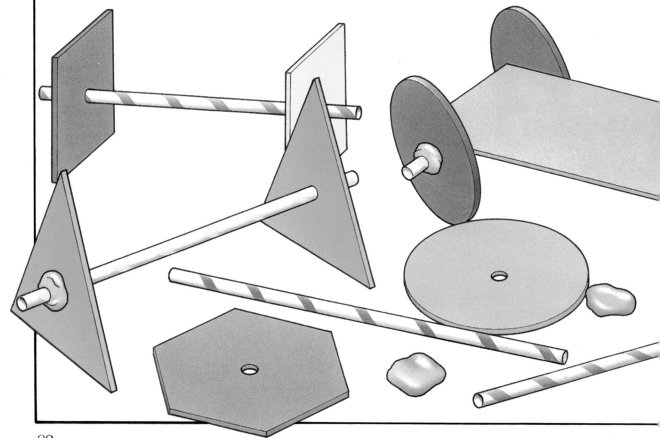

▲ The wheel is one of the most important inventions ever made. No one knows who invented the wheel but it has been used for thousands of years. This mosaic of a Sumerian cart is nearly 4,500 years old.

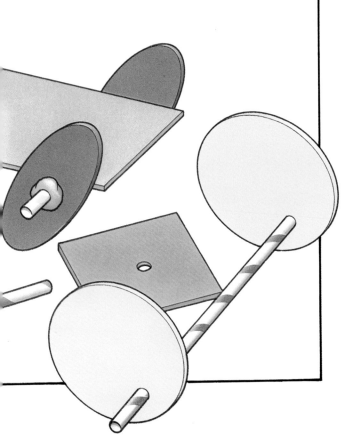

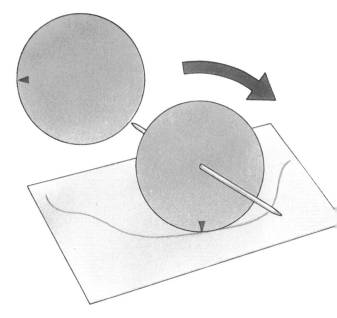

Wheels for Measuring

Wheels can be used for measuring distances. Make a measuring wheel yourself. Cut out a circle of cardboard and push a toothpick through the middle. Make a mark on the edge of the wheel. Lay your wheel on a piece of paper and use the mark to help you measure the distance the wheel takes to turn around once.

How far do you go for one turn of your bicycle wheel? Ask a friend to help you measure the distance.

Tie a handkerchief around the tire

◀ Trains run on wheels with a sloping edge, like an ice cream cone. This shape helps the train to stay on the track. These children are experimenting with different shaped wheels to see which ones are best at staying on the track.

Real train wheels have a special edge called a flange, which helps to keep the engine and coaches from falling off the track.

Wheels for Lifting

A wheel with a groove for carrying a rope is called a pulley. By pulling down on the rope, we can lift heavy things. Look out for pulleys in cranes, in lifts, on sailing ships, and on some washing lines.

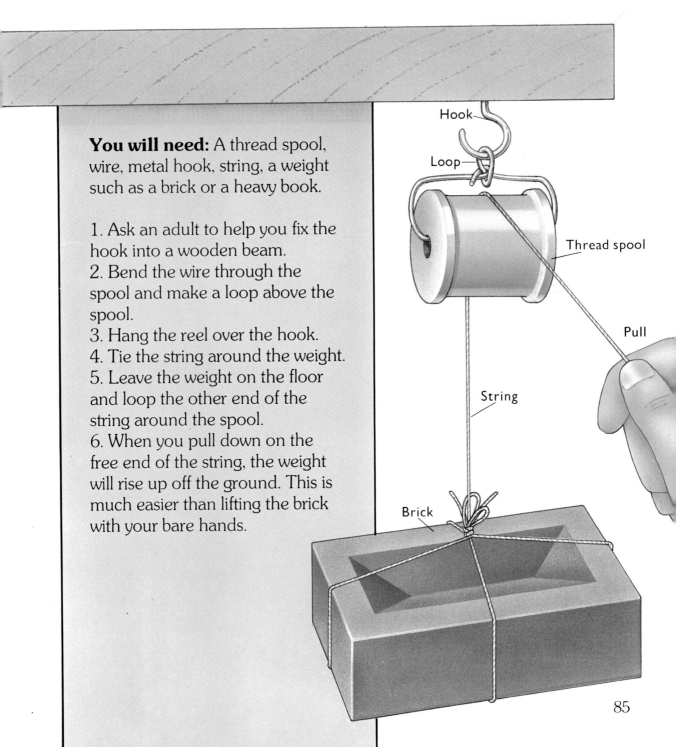

You will need: A thread spool, wire, metal hook, string, a weight such as a brick or a heavy book.

1. Ask an adult to help you fix the hook into a wooden beam.
2. Bend the wire through the spool and make a loop above the spool.
3. Hang the reel over the hook.
4. Tie the string around the weight.
5. Leave the weight on the floor and loop the other end of the string around the spool.
6. When you pull down on the free end of the string, the weight will rise up off the ground. This is much easier than lifting the brick with your bare hands.

Hook

Loop

Thread spool

Pull

String

Brick

Wheels with Teeth

A wheel with teeth around the edge is called a gear wheel. To make a gear wheel, cut two circles of cardboard. Make a hole through the middle of both circles. Stick pieces of thin wood onto one piece of cardboard. Arrange them in a wheel shape so the end of the wood sticks out around the edge of the circle. Stick the other circle on top.

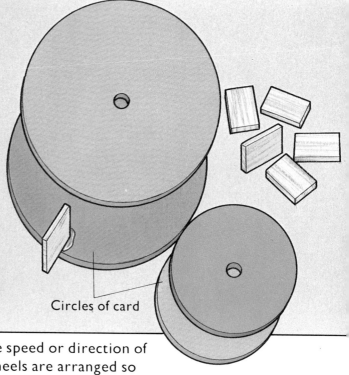

Circles of card

▼ Gear wheels are used to change the speed or direction of movement. Inside a clock, the gear wheels are arranged so they make the big hand and the little hand turn at different speeds.

To start with, make one big wheel and one small wheel. Push a pencil through the middle of each wheel and push the pencil through a large piece of cardboard. Arrange the gear wheels so the teeth link together.

Turn the big wheel once. Which way does the small wheel turn? How many times does the small wheel turn around? Does the small wheel turn faster or slower than the big wheel?

Handle

Handle

To make a gear machine, make different sized wheels with different numbers of teeth. Arrange them to match the picture. When you turn one gear wheel, what happens to the other wheels?

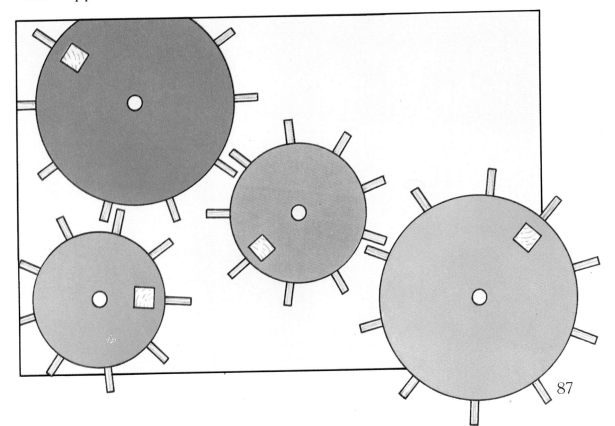

STOP AND GO

Have you ever been in a car that stopped suddenly? The sudden force throws you forward after the car has stopped. A seat belt keeps you in your seat so you don't hit the seats or the windshield.

You are thrown forward because of something called inertia. Inertia is a physical property that keeps moving things moving, or stationary things still—unless a strong force acts on them. The word inertia comes from the Latin word for laziness.

Flick the Paper

Put a plastic mug on a piece of paper. Can you pull the paper out from under the mug without knocking it over?

The trick is to pull the paper out very sharply. The mug will be left behind because the pulling force is not strong enough to overcome its inertia. Can you repeat the trick with a mug full of water?

In a Spin

Find two table tennis balls and make a small hole in each one. Make up some jello and pour the liquid jello into one of the balls. Leave the jello to set hard. Pour water into the other ball. Put tape across the holes.

Now spin each ball in turn on a smooth surface. Stop the ball with your fingers and then let go. What happens?

Snapping Strings

Put about a pound of small stones or marbles into a small plastic bag. Tie a long piece of thread to the top of the bag and another piece of thread to the bottom of the bag. Rest a stick or broom handle over two chairs and tie the top thread to the stick. Pull the bottom thread sharply. What happens?

Now tie another piece of thread to the bottom of the bag. Pull the bottom thread slowly. What happens this time?

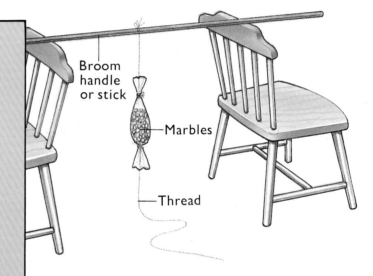

Broom handle or stick

Marbles

Thread

What happens
The water ball will start spinning again when you let go. Inertia keeps the water swirling around inside the ball and this starts the ball spinning again. There is no movement inside the jello ball. So when you stop it spinning, it stays still. You can use this trick to help you tell the difference between a raw egg and a cooked egg.

What happens
When you pull the bottom thread sharply, the inertia of the stones stops the pull from reaching the top thread. So the bottom thread snaps. When you pull the bottom thread slowly, the steady pull is a strong enough force to overcome the inertia of the stones. This time, the pull reaches the top thread and it snaps first.

STICKING AND SLIPPING

Rub your hands together very quickly. The heat you feel is caused by a force called friction. Friction tries to stop things sliding past each other and slows things down. Without friction, we would slip over every time we tried to walk.

Science Friction

To find out more about the friction on different surfaces, try these tests.

You will need:
A table, a tablecloth, carpet tiles, sandpaper, shiny hardboard, newspaper, string, scissors, a wooden block, a yogurt pot, marbles, a hook.

1. To protect the table, cover it with an old cloth or blanket.
2. Fit the hook into one side of the wooden block.
3. Tie one end of the string to the yogurt pot and the other end to the hook.

4. Put each surface onto the table in turn.
5. Put the block on top of the surface.
6. To make the block move, how many marbles do you need to put in the yogurt pot?

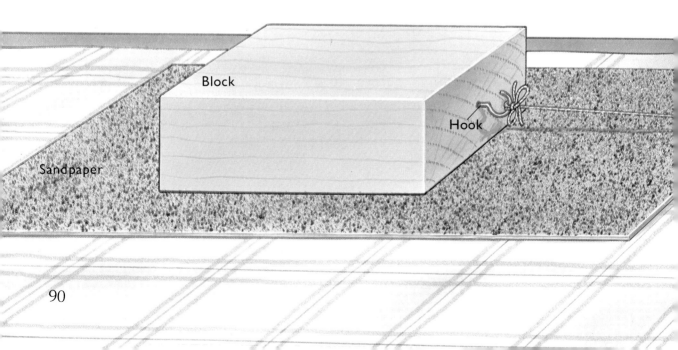

Block

Hook

Sandpaper

▲ Skis are very narrow so that only a small surface comes into contact with the snow. They are also smooth underneath. This reduces the amount of friction between the skis and the snow and helps skiers to slide at high speeds over the snow.

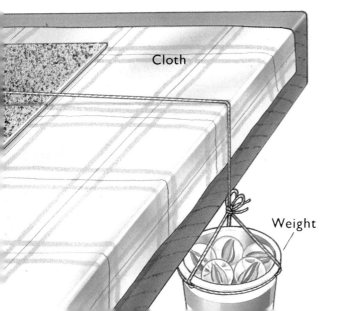

Cloth

Weight

What happens

The rough surfaces cause more friction. You need more marbles in the pot to overcome this friction and make the block move. Which surface causes the most friction?

Braking Power

A lot of friction can sometimes be useful. Bicycle brakes work because of friction. When you squeeze the brakes, rubber or plastic pads press against the wheel rims and stop the wheels turning.

Next time you brake hard, stop and feel the wheel rim. It will be warm because of friction.

Too much Friction

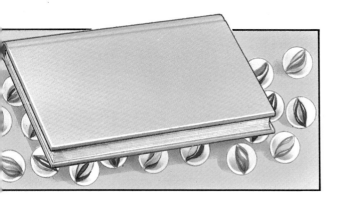

Try pushing a book along the carpet. Friction stops the book sliding along easily. Now put some marbles under the book and push it again. This time it moves easily because the marbles roll and cut down the friction.

Sometimes, friction is a problem. In machines, it makes moving parts get hot and wear out more quickly. It also wastes energy. Ball bearings are used to help the moving parts inside machines spin more easily. A bearing is often made of a ring of smooth, shiny balls which roll around in a groove between the fixed and the moving parts of a machine. This reduces friction.

Ball bearings

Make a Hovercraft

A hovercraft floats above the ground or the water on a cushion of air. This cuts down the amount of friction and helps the hovercraft to move more easily.

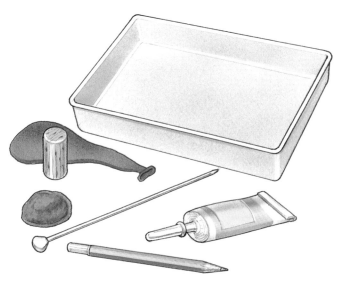

You will need: a balloon, a polystyrene food tray, a small cork, glue, a knitting needle, modeling clay, a pencil.

1. Ask an adult to use the knitting needle to make a hole through the middle of the cork.
2. Use the pencil to make a small hole in the middle of the food tray.
3. Glue the cork to the bottom of the tray so the holes are lined up.
4. Put modeling clay around the cork to stop air escaping.
5. Put the tray on a smooth surface.
6. Blow up the balloon. Hold the end tightly so the air can't get out and fit the nozzle of the balloon over the cork.
7. Give the tray a gentle push and it should glide away.

What happens

The air from the balloon rushes down through the cork and out under the tray. The air lifts the tray a little way off the floor. When you push your hovercraft, it glides along on this layer of air, just like a real hovercraft.

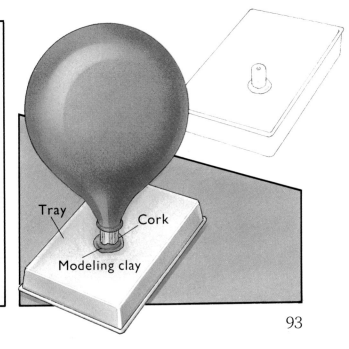

Tray

Cork

Modeling clay

It is easier to pull a heavy weight up a slope than to lift it straight up. Prove this for yourself. Tie a piece of string around a stone and tie a rubber band to the string. To make a slope, pile up several books and rest a ruler against the books. Use the rubber band to pull the stone up the ruler. How far does the band stretch?

Now take away the ruler and lift the stone straight up from the floor to the top of the books. Does the elastic band stretch farther this time?

Elastic band

Stone

Ruler

 **Sliding down Slopes**

Tie a piece of string to a heavy object, such as a book or a brick. Pull the string through a large clip. Tie the other end of the string to a handle or fixed bar. Put the clip at the top of the slope. How long does it take to slide down? Change the angle of the slope. How does this change the speed of the clip? Try sliding other objects, such as rolls of tape or paper clips, down your slope. How does the size and weight of the object affect its speed down the slope?

Bulldog clip

Rolled-up-Slopes

Screws can be used to lift things, press things, or force things apart. A screw holds two pieces of wood together more firmly than a nail.

A screw is really a rolled-up slope. You can check this idea for yourself. Draw a slope on a piece of paper and cut it out. Then wind the paper around a pencil. Compare this with a real screw.

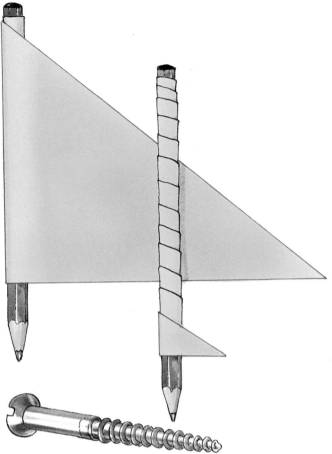

Did you know that a wedge is two slopes joined back-to-back? An ax is a kind of wedge. If you push a wedge into a gap, you force the load past its sloping sides. This makes it easier to force things apart.

This edge of a screw is called a thread.

▶ This model of an Archimedes screw is being used to lift grain up out of a pit into a hopper. This machine was invented thousands of years ago by the Greek scientist Archimedes. In Egypt, it is still used to lift water for irrigation.

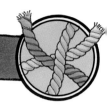

STRETCH AND TWIST

Pull some of the skin on your arm. How far will your skin stretch? What happens when you let go? Materials that stretch but go back to their original shape are called elastic materials.

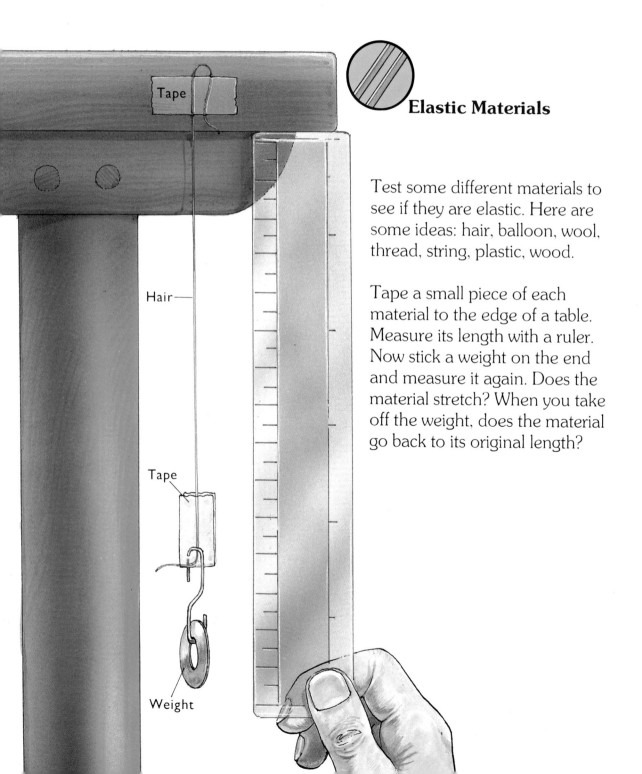

Elastic Materials

Test some different materials to see if they are elastic. Here are some ideas: hair, balloon, wool, thread, string, plastic, wood.

Tape a small piece of each material to the edge of a table. Measure its length with a ruler. Now stick a weight on the end and measure it again. Does the material stretch? When you take off the weight, does the material go back to its original length?

Tape

Hair

Tape

Weight

Make a Weighing Machine

Rubber is an elastic material. You can use a rubber band to make a weighing machine.

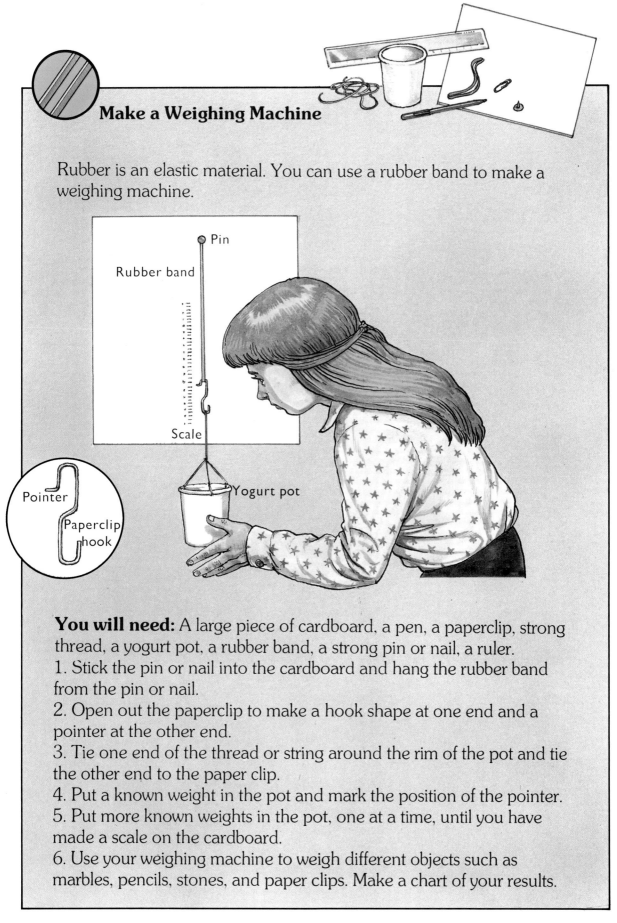

You will need: A large piece of cardboard, a pen, a paperclip, strong thread, a yogurt pot, a rubber band, a strong pin or nail, a ruler.

1. Stick the pin or nail into the cardboard and hang the rubber band from the pin or nail.
2. Open out the paperclip to make a hook shape at one end and a pointer at the other end.
3. Tie one end of the thread or string around the rim of the pot and tie the other end to the paper clip.
4. Put a known weight in the pot and mark the position of the pointer.
5. Put more known weights in the pot, one at a time, until you have made a scale on the cardboard.
6. Use your weighing machine to weigh different objects such as marbles, pencils, stones, and paper clips. Make a chart of your results.

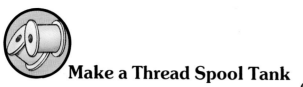

Make a Thread Spool Tank

This tank rolls along using the energy from a twisted rubber band.

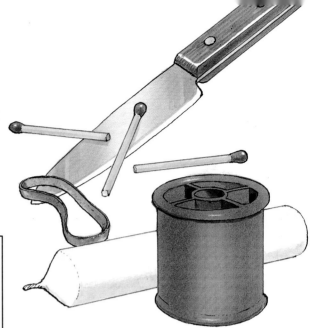

You will need: A thread spool, a small rubber band, three matchsticks, a candle, a ruler, a knife.

Ask an adult to help you with the first three steps.

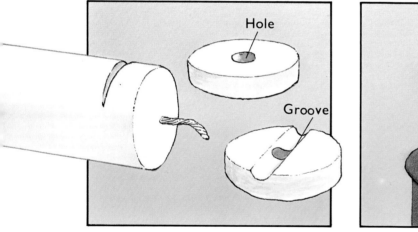

Hole

Groove

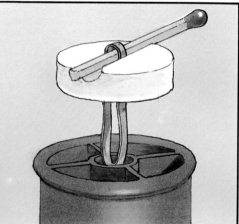

1. Cut a thin slice of wax from the candle.
2. Use the knife to make a hole in the middle of the slice.
3. Make a groove in one side of the slice straight across the middle.
4. Push the rubber band through the hole in the slice and put a matchstick through the band. Pull the band so the matchstick is held in the groove.
5. Pull the other end of the band through the hole in the middle of the spool.
6. Push half a matchstick through the band to hold it in place.
7. Push another matchstick into one of the holes through the reel. This will stop the half matchstick from turning around.
8. To twist the rubber band, turn the matchstick in the groove around several times.
9. When you put your tank on the floor or on a table, the band will slowly unwind and push the tank along.
10. You could have a tank race with your friends.

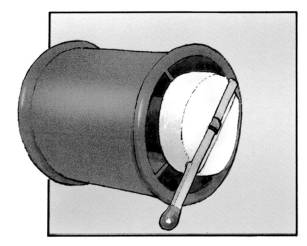 

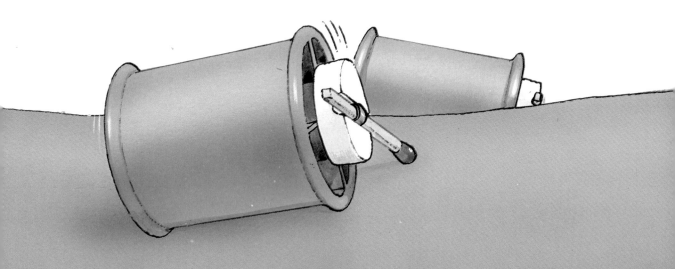

If you throw a ball up in the air, it falls back down to the ground. This happens because of a force called gravity, which pulls things down to the ground. The Earth is so big that the pull of its gravity is very strong. It keeps everything on the Earth. We rely on gravity to pour drinks, mail letters, or drill holes. Without gravity, everything on Earth would fly off into space.

These astronauts are learning to cope with the "weightless" feeling they will experience out in Space. On Earth, we have weight because gravity pulls us down to the ground.

Falling Forces

To see how gravity affects falling objects, try these tests.

You will need: newspaper, large sheets of paper, a straw or eyedropper, tape, thin paint or ink.

1. Put lots of newspaper on the floor.
2. Tape a sheet of paper on top of the newspaper.
3. Pick up some of the thin paint or ink with the straw or eye dropper.
4. Drop the paint or ink from a height of 6 inches, 12 inches, 20 inches, and 40 inches.
5. Before you let each drop fall, guess the size of the blob it will make on the paper.
6. What happens if you drop thicker paint or ink from the same heights?

To make a straw dropper

Hold your finger over the end of a straw. Dip it into the paint or ink. The paint or ink will not fall out until you take your finger off the end of the straw.

What happens

When the paint or ink drops fall from a greater height, gravity makes them fall faster. They are traveling at a faster speed when they hit the ground, so they make bigger marks on the paper.

Anti-gravity Cones

The cones in this investigation seem to roll uphill, against the force of gravity. How is this possible?

1. Cut two pieces of cardboard to match the shape in the picture.
2. Tape the two shortest sides of the cardboard together.
3. Hold the paper by one of the corners on the long side. Make a cone shape by curling the other corner on the long side around your hand. Ask a friend to help you tape the paper to hold it in place.
4. Use scissors to trim the point off the open end of the cone to make a circle.
5. Make another cone exactly the same size and shape. Tape the open ends of the cones together to match the picture.
6. Put the paper cones at the bottom of the hill and watch them climb upward.

You will need:

Cardboard, plain paper about 8 inches by 5 inches, a pencil, a ruler, scissors, tape.

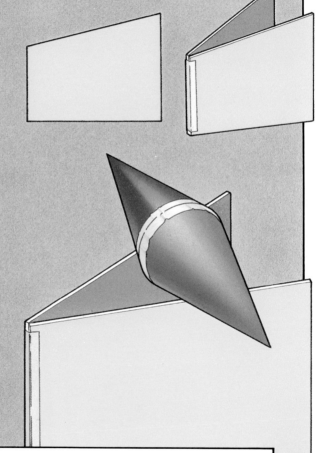

What happens

The middle part of the cones really goes downhill. So the cones are not going against the force of gravity. You can prove this by measuring the distance from the middle of the cones to the ground when they are at the top of the hill. At this point, the cones will be lower down than at the bottom of the hill.

Machines need energy to make them work. This power can come from gasoline, electricity, and the pushing force of water or the wind. Can you think of any other sources of energy for machines?

Make a Windmill

You will need:
A piece of colored paper about 6 inches square, scissors, a pin, a bead, a stick.

1. Cut lines in the piece of paper to match the picture.
2. Fold in the pieces marked with a cross.
3. Push the pin through the middle of the folded pieces.
4. Thread a bead on to the back of a pin.
5. Ask an adult to help you push the pin into a stick.
6. On a windy day, put the windmill outside and see how fast it turns around.

Windmills can be used to grind flour or raise water from a well. Nowadays, special windmills are used to make electricity. This does not pollute the environment, but it is only possible in places where there are a lot of strong winds.

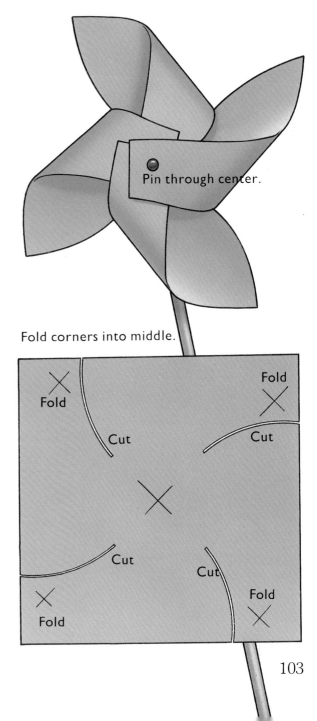

Pin through center.

Fold corners into middle.

Fold · Cut · Fold · Cut · Fold · Cut · Cut · Fold

103

TRUE OR FALSE?

1 Scissors and see-saws are both kinds of lever.

2 Smooth surfaces cause more friction.

3 A screw is a rolled-up slope.

4 Elastic materials stretch but do not go back to their original size and shape.

5 On Earth, things have weight because gravity pulls them down to the ground.

6 In a clock, gear wheels make the big hand and the little hand turn at the same speed.

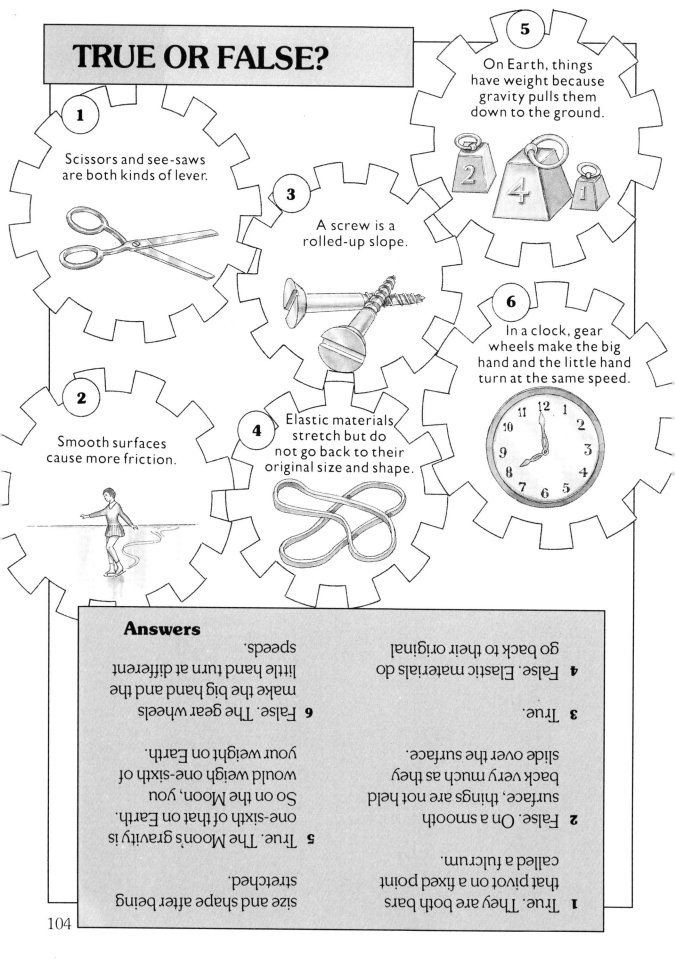

Answers

1 True. They are both bars that pivot on a fixed point called a fulcrum.

2 False. On a smooth surface, things are not held back very much as they slide over the surface.

3 True.

4 False. Elastic materials do go back to their original size and shape after being stretched.

5 True. The Moon's gravity is one-sixth of that on Earth. So on the Moon, you would weigh one-sixth of your weight on Earth.

6 False. The gear wheels make the big hand and the little hand turn at different speeds.

Sound
and
Music

Does sound travel faster through water or through air?
How many decibels is normal conversation? How do
stethoscopes help doctors to hear inside the human body?
If you blow across the top of a short straw, does it produce
a higher or a lower note than a long straw? How do
recorders produce lots of different notes? Why are two ears
better than one?

This section will help you to discover the answers to these
questions and has lots of ideas for ways to investigate
sound and music.

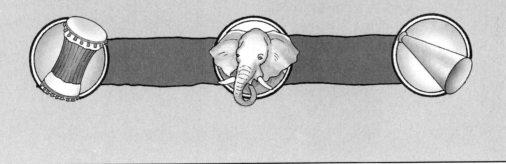

SOUND AND MUSIC

In this section, you can discover how we hear sounds and find out how to make music by plucking strings, blowing down pipes, and hitting percussion instruments, such as drums.

The section is divided into seven different topics. Look out for the big headings with a circle at each end — like the one at the top of this page. These headings tell you where a new topic starts.

Pages 108–111 **Sounds all Around**

Everyday sounds; what is sound?; how sound travels through solids, water or air.

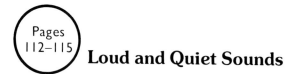

Pages 112–115 **Loud and Quiet Sounds**

Decibel scale; testing your hearing; megaphones and stethoscopes.

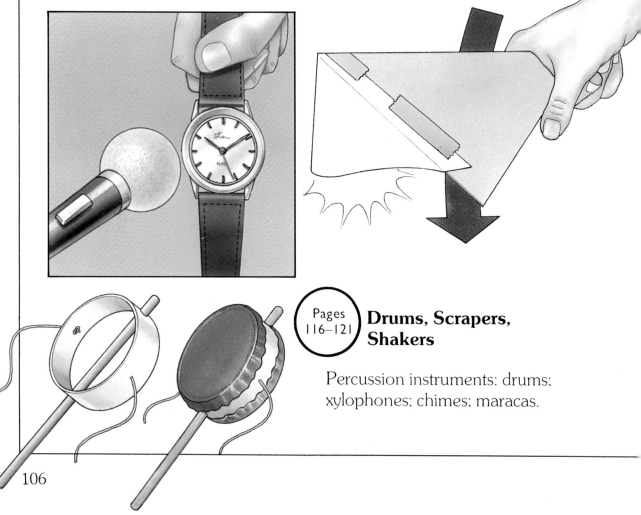

Pages 116–121 **Drums, Scrapers, Shakers**

Percussion instruments: drums; xylophones; chimes; maracas.

Music from Pipes

Pages 122–127

Organs; Pan pipes; recorders; trumpets; trombones.

Music from Strings

Pages 128–131

Pianos; guitars; violins.

Making Music

Pages 132–133

Instruments in an orchestra.

Sound Messages

Pages 134–135

Sirens; telephones; animal sounds.

SOUNDS ALL AROUND

Make a tape recording of the everyday sounds around you. You could include sounds such as a door banging, a clock ticking, a bell ringing, or the sounds made by people, pets, or traffic. Try to record sounds indoors and out of doors.

Play the tape back to a friend. Can they recognize all the different sounds? Can you think of words to describe the sounds? Make up a poem or a story which includes all the sounds on the tape.

▶ In a noisy place, such as a fairground, it is hard to pick out individual sounds.

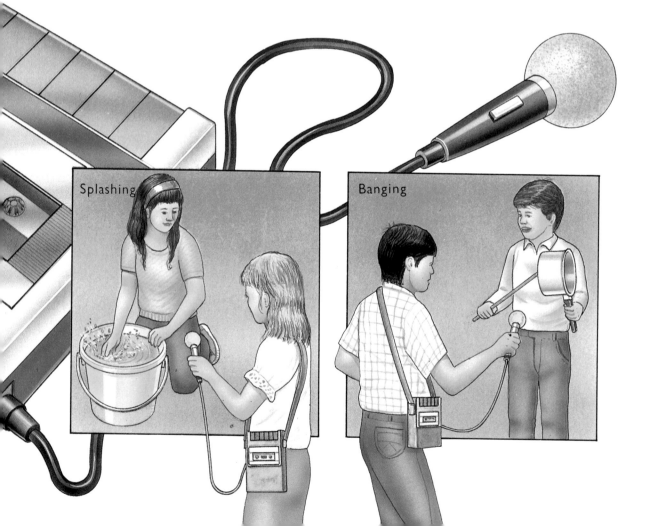

Splashing

Banging

Rustling

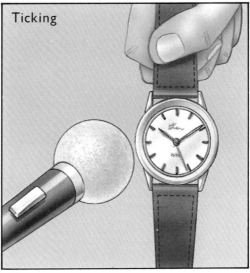

Ticking

Making Sounds

Make a collection of different materials, such as tissue paper, sandpaper, foil, cardboard, wood, plastic, sponge, and glass. Put up a screen and ask your friends to sit on one side of the screen. On the other side of the screen, make sounds with the materials in your collection. How many different ways of making sounds can you discover? Can your friends guess which materials you are using each time?

Sound on the Move

Find a long length of iron railings and ask a friend to stand at one end while you stand at the other end. When your friend taps the railings with a stick, can you hear the sound? Now put your ear close to the railings and repeat the experiment. What happens to the sound?

Sounds Underwater

Blow up a balloon and hold it next to your ear. Hold a watch on the other side of the balloon. Can you hear the watch ticking? Now fill the balloon with water and repeat the experiment. Does the water make the sound louder or quieter?

Sound travels about four times faster through water than it does through air. The sound of the watch should be louder through the water-filled balloon.

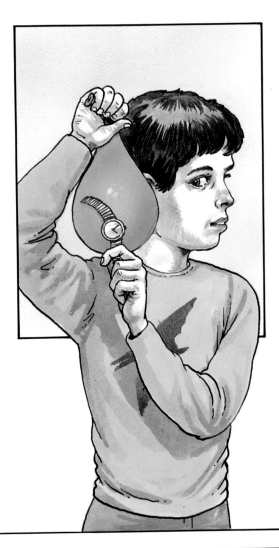

What Happens
Sounds travel faster through solid materials, such as the iron railings, than they do through air. So when you put your ear to the railings, the sound seems much louder. Try the same experiment with a brick wall instead of iron railings. You could make up a code of long and short taps and send messages.

111

LOUD AND QUIET SOUNDS

What is the loudest sound you have ever heard? Was it made by an airplane, a siren, or thunder during a storm? How many quiet sounds can you think of? Here are some ideas to get you started: footsteps on the carpet, a ticking watch, a mouse squeaking.

Draw a chart of objects that make loud sounds and objects that make quiet sounds. Do the objects in each group have anything in common?

The loudness of a sound is measured in units called decibels. Here is the decibel scale *(right).* Did you know that a humpback whale can make a noise louder than a jet plane on take-off? (190 decibels)

Decibel Scale	
0	humans can just hear sounds
10	rustling leaves
20	whisper
60	normal conversation
80	heavy traffic
100	jackhammer
110	discotheque
120	jet airplane

▶ We call sounds we don't want or don't like noise. Very loud noise can damage our ears. People who work in noisy places should wear ear muffs to protect their ears.

Make your own ear muffs from foil cake cases or empty boxes. Hold them over your ears or use a hair band, rubber bands, or shoe laces to fix them in position. To cut out even more noise, try padding out the inside of the ear muffs with cotton balls, or tissue paper.

Make a Paper Snapper

You will need:

a square piece of cardboard
8 inches by 8 inches, a piece
of paper 5 inches by 5 inches,
scissors, a ruler, sticky tape.

1. Draw a line half an inch away from the edge
on two sides of the paper to match the picture. Cut across the paper
diagonally, making sure both lined edges are on one side of the scissors.
Throw away the paper without the lines on it.

2. Put one corner of the cardboard onto the paper up against the two
lines. Fold the paper along the lines over the cardboard. Fasten the
paper in place using sticky tape.

3. Turn the snapper over and fold it in half diagonally so most of the
paper is inside. Grip the fold of the snapper firmly in the palm of your
hand, with the taped side at the top. Now pull the snapper quickly
down through the air and flick your wrist to make the paper snap out of
the cardboard.

Making Sounds Louder

Cup your hands and hold them behind your ears. Can you hear better with your big ears? Now try holding your hands in front of your ears with the palms facing backward. Can you hear the sounds behind you more easily? How many animals can you think of with big ears?

Make a Stethoscope

Push a plastic funnel onto each end of a long piece of plastic or rubber tubing. Then ask a friend to hold one funnel over their chest while you hold the other funnel to your ear. Can you hear your friend's heart beating?
A doctor uses a stethoscope like this to listen to sounds inside the body. This helps the doctor to find out about a person's health.

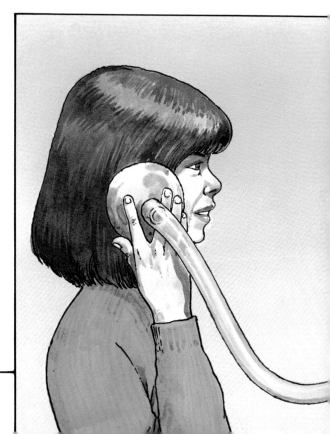

Making a Trumpet . . . and a Megaphone

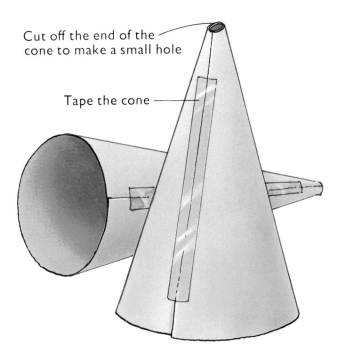

Cut off the end of the cone to make a small hole

Tape the cone

Make an ear trumpet by rolling a large sheet of paper into a cone shape. Hold the thin end of the trumpet to your ear. The cone collects sounds and makes them seem louder. With an ear trumpet in each ear, can you hear twice as well? Do large trumpets work better than small ones? How many musical instruments can you think of which include a trumpet?

To make a megaphone, shout into the narrow end. The cone makes your voice seem louder.
Ask a friend to shout into a megaphone while you listen with an ear trumpet. How far away can you hear the sound of your friend's voice?

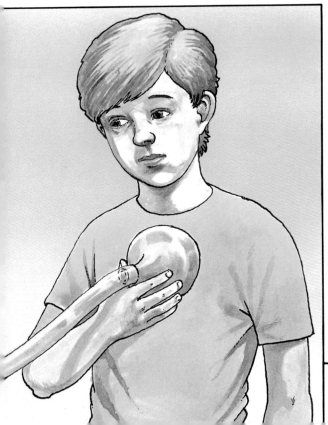

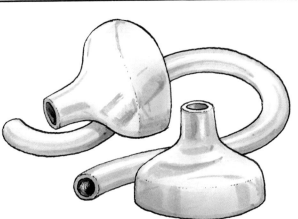

Instead of funnels, ask an adult to cut off the tops of two plastic bottles, as shown here.

DRUMS, SCRAPERS, SHAKERS

Many musical instruments produce sounds when they are hit. These are called percussion instruments. The name comes from the word "percuss," which means to strike. They include drums, cymbals, triangles, tambourines, and xylophones.

 **Making Drums**

You can use a box or any hollow container as a drum. To make a drum that gives out different notes, you need a drum skin. Cut a piece out of a plastic bag and stretch it over a plastic bowl. Use tape or string to hold the bag in place. If you stretch the skin tighter, the plastic skin will vibrate faster and make a higher note.

Try making a drumskin from different materials, such as cloth, a balloon, or paper soaked in wallpaper paste to make it go hard. Which materials make the best sounds? Which materials last longest?

Try putting a few grains of rice on top of the drum. When you tap the drum, the sound makes the drum shake and the rice jumps up in the air. When the drum skin is stretched tighter, does the rice jump higher in the air?

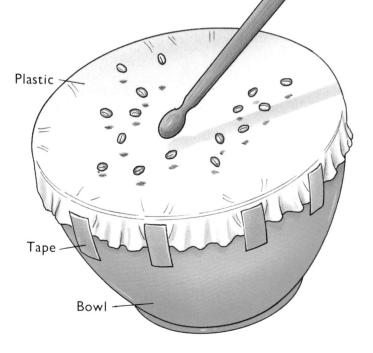

Plastic

Tape

Bowl

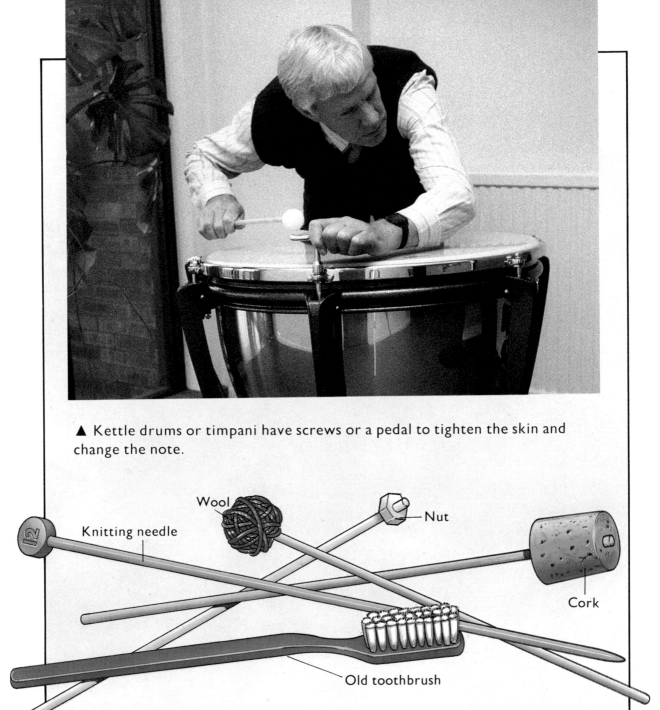

▲ Kettle drums or timpani have screws or a pedal to tighten the skin and change the note.

Wool

Nut

Knitting needle

Cork

Old toothbrush

Making Drumsticks

You can make different sounds with the same drum by using different ends on the drumsticks. Here are some ideas to try:
wooden beads, cork, a cloth, wool, sponge, a nut, bristles from a toothbrush or a hairbrush.

Fix the ends to the drumsticks with tape or rubber bands. Cloth or sponge ends make a quiet sound. Beads make a louder sound. What sort of sound do the bristles make? Which sound do you like best?

Making Scrapers

A plastic bottle with ridges along the sides makes a good scraper. Try using different objects, such as metal spoons, pencils, or stones to scrape along the ridges.

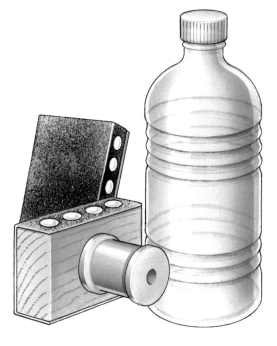

You can make another kind of scraper from two wooden blocks with sandpaper pinned on top. To make a handle for each scraper, glue a thread spool to the back of the block. Paint the backs of the scrapers with bright patterns. To make scraping sounds, hold one block in each hand and rub the sandpaper sides together.

Make different sized pairs of scrapers. How are the sounds different? Try sticking the sandpaper to hollow boxes instead of solid blocks of wood. You should be able to make louder sounds.

Make a Nail Xylophone

Ask an adult to help you bang some nails into a piece of wood so they stick out at different heights. Tap each nail with a metal spoon. Which nail makes the highest note? Which nail makes the lowest note?

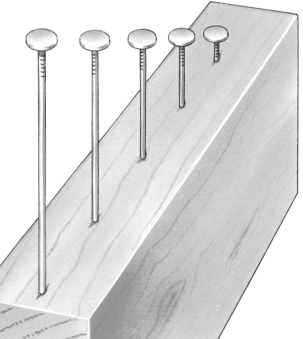

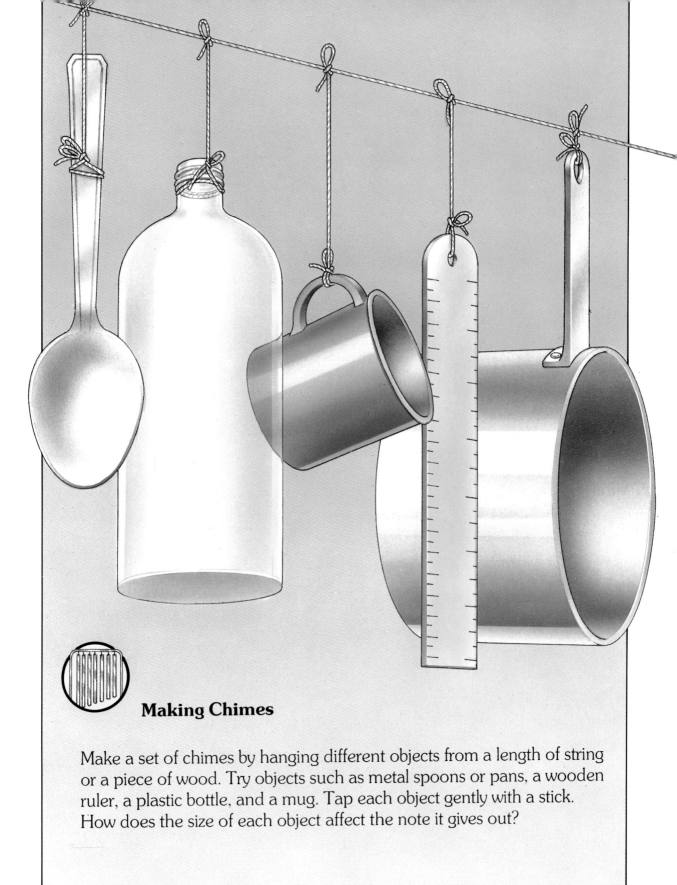

Making Chimes

Make a set of chimes by hanging different objects from a length of string or a piece of wood. Try objects such as metal spoons or pans, a wooden ruler, a plastic bottle, and a mug. Tap each object gently with a stick. How does the size of each object affect the note it gives out?

Shake, Rattle, and Roll

A shaker can be made from empty plastic bottles, margarine cartons, or small boxes. Collect containers that are different shapes and sizes and make sure they are clean and dry inside. Fill each container with small objects that will rattle around inside.

Fix the lid on the container with sticky tape and paint your shaker or cover it with wrapping paper. Which fillings make the loudest sound?

Here are some ideas for the fillings:

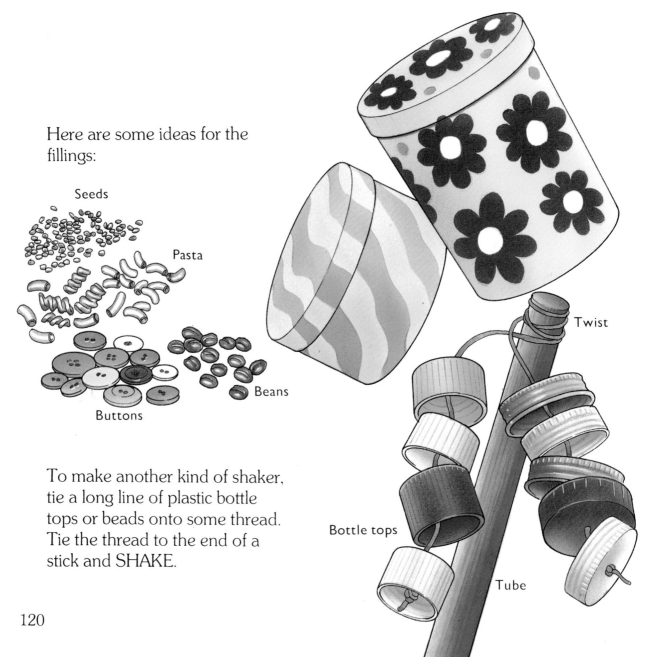

Seeds

Pasta

Beans

Buttons

Bottle tops

Twist

Tube

To make another kind of shaker, tie a long line of plastic bottle tops or beads onto some thread. Tie the thread to the end of a stick and SHAKE.

Making Maracas

1. Make small cuts around one end of the tube so it opens out flat. Glue this end to the bottom of one of the cups.
2. Pour the beans into the other cup.
3. Fix the two cups firmly together with plenty of sticky tape so the beans can't escape.
4. Paint or color the cardboard tube.
5. Hold the cardboard tube and shake to make a sound.
6. Make another one and shake your maracas in time with your favorite music.

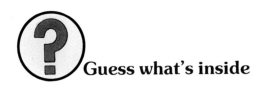

Cups

Tube

You will need:

two paper cups, a cardboard tube, dried beans, scissors, sticky tape, glue, paints or crayons.

Guess what's inside

Find a bottle you can't see through and choose one sort of filling to put inside. Can your friends guess what is inside the shaker?

If you blow across the top of an empty bottle, you can make a musical note. This happens because you are making the air inside the bottle shake or vibrate. Musical instruments such as recorders, organs, or trumpets work in a similar way. The player blows into the end of a pipe and this makes the air vibrate and give out musical sounds.

Make a Bottle Organ

1. Collect several clean, glass bottles that are all the same size and shape.
2. Put the bottles in a line.
3. Fill one bottle with water almost to the top. Leave some air above the water.
4. Put a little less water in the next bottle and so on down the line. The last bottle should have just a small amount of water in the bottom.
5. Blow across the top of each bottle. Which bottle makes the highest note? Which bottle makes the lowest note?
6. With a metal spoon, tap each bottle gently. What happens to the notes?
7. Can you play a tune on your bottles? It is a good idea to put a number on each bottle. Then you can write down your music.

 **Singing Bottles**

Find two clean, empty glass bottles that are exactly the same size and shape. Ask a friend to hold one of the bottles to their ear. Then stand about a yard away and blow across the top of the other bottle. What can your friend hear?

The vibrations of the air in your bottle trigger the same vibrations in your friend's bottle. So they should hear a faint note in their bottle. This is called resonance.

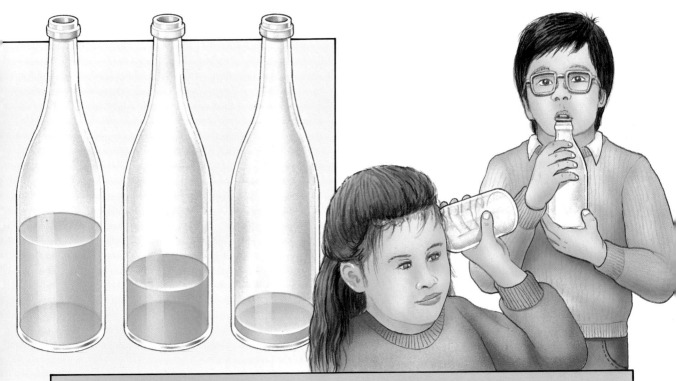

What Happens

When you blow across a bottle with a small amount of air inside, the air vibrates quickly and makes a high note. With more air in the bottle, the air vibrates more slowly and the note is lower.

When you tap the bottles, you make the water vibrate instead of the air. So the notes are the opposite way round. The bottles with a small amount of water give out high notes and the bottles with a lot of water give out low notes.

 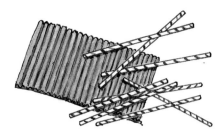

Make Pan Pipes

Pan pipes are a set of pipes that are played by blowing across the top. They are named for the Greek god Pan, who was half man and half goat. The music from his pipes was supposed to have power over all animals. The organ was probably developed from Pan pipes.

You will need:
a thin strip of corrugated cardboard, eight straws, scissors.

1. Push a straw through every other opening in the cardboard.
2. Cut each straw a different length with the longest straw at one end and the shortest straw at the other end. Make sure you have an even, sloping line, which matches the picture.
3. To play your Pan pipes, blow across the tops of the straws. Which straw makes the highest note? Which straw makes the lowest note?

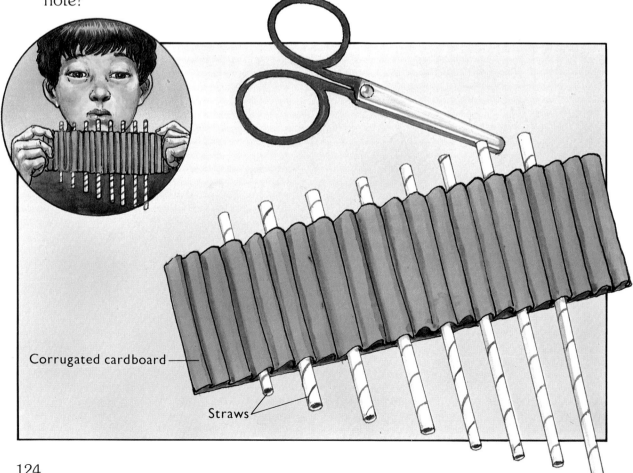

Corrugated cardboard

Straws

▲ If one pipe makes one note, how do instruments such as recorders make lots of different notes? A recorder has small holes at intervals along the pipe. When the player covers all the holes with their fingers, they are using one long pipe. When they take one or more fingers off the holes, they make the pipe shorter. This means they can play different notes.

Sound from Grass

Blade of grass

Hold a thick blade of grass tightly between your thumbs and blow hard. Can you make a screeching noise? The grass vibrates to produce the sound. This is what happens when a person blows on a reed in a musical instrument. Such instruments were originally all made of wood, and they are all played by the breath of the person, so they are called woodwind instruments.

Musical Straws

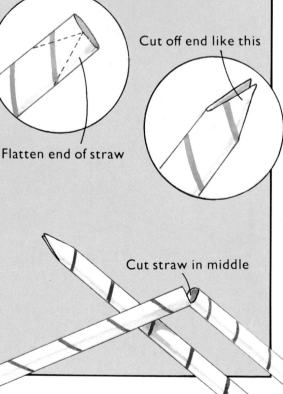

Cut off end like this

Flatten end of straw

Cut straw in middle

1. Flatten the end of a straw and snip the end to make two points or "reeds." Now blow hard between the two reeds to set the air in the straw vibrating.
2. Keep blowing through the reeds while you snip off bits from the other end of the straw. What happens to the note?
3. To make a straw play two notes, cut a hole in one side of the middle of the straw. Bend the straw down to play a different note.

Make a Trombone

Purse your lips and make a noise down a piece of plastic piping. Keep making the noise as you lift the pipe up and down in a bucket of water. How does the sound change?

A real trombone player pushes a slide on the side of the instrument up and down to change the length of the tube.

▼ Instruments made from brass, such as this trumpet, do not have reeds inside them. Instead, the player uses his own lips as reeds. When his lips are pressed tightly together, the air vibrates rapidly and produces a high note. He makes lower notes with his lips pressed loosely together.

MUSIC FROM STRINGS

Stretch a rubber band around a book and put two pencils under the band. Pluck the band to make it vibrate and produce a sound. First try with the pencils a long way apart. Then move the pencils closer together. With a shorter length of band to vibrate, you will produce a higher note.

Musical instruments that produce sound by vibrating strings are called stringed instruments. Some, such as the guitar, are played with the fingers. Others, such as the violin, are played with a bow.

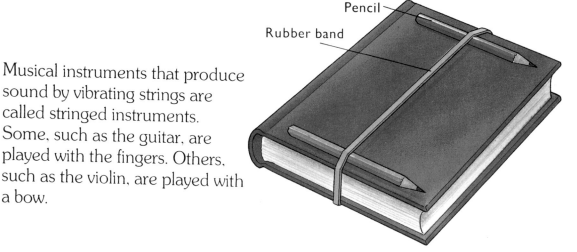

Pencil
Rubber band

Pinging Strings

1. Ask an adult to help you knock the nails into the wood to match the picture.
2. Pull one elastic band around each pair of nails.
3. Pluck the elastic bands with your fingers. Which bands make high sounds? Which bands make low sounds?

Nails
Rubber band

You will need:

a thick piece of wood, a hammer, some short nails, six rubber bands all the same size and thickness.

 **Make a Guitar**

Collect together a large plastic box and eight rubber bands. Try to find long and short bands as well as thick and thin ones. Stretch the bands around the box and pluck them to make musical notes. Do the thin bands make higher or lower notes than the thick bands? If you use a bigger box or a smaller box, how does this change the notes?

What Happens

The vibrations of the bands make the air inside the box vibrate. And this, in turn, makes a lot of air around the box vibrate too. So you hear louder notes than from a solid piece of wood. This is why instruments with strings have a hollow box underneath the strings.

Rubber band

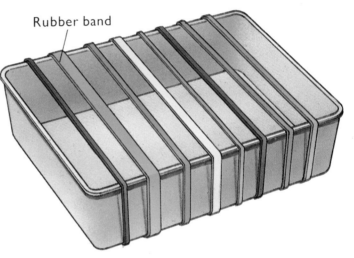

▼ Did you know that a piano makes music by vibrating strings? When the piano keys are pressed, little hammers hit wires inside the piano. This makes the wires and the whole piano case vibrate. The piano case makes the air around the piano vibrate too so it works like a giant sound box.

Stretching Strings

You will need:

a piece of wood, a nail, a hammer, string, a small plastic bucket, marbles or stones, two pencils.

1. Ask an adult to help you hammer the nail into the wood to match the picture.
2. Tie one end of the string to the nail.
3. Ask an adult to hold the piece of wood securely on a table. Put some marbles or stones into the bucket and tie this to the other end of the string.
4. Put the pencils underneath the string to lift it clear of the wood.
5. Pluck the string and listen to the note.
6. Now put some more marbles or stones into the bucket so the string is stretched tighter.
7. Pluck the string again. Is the note higher or lower this time?

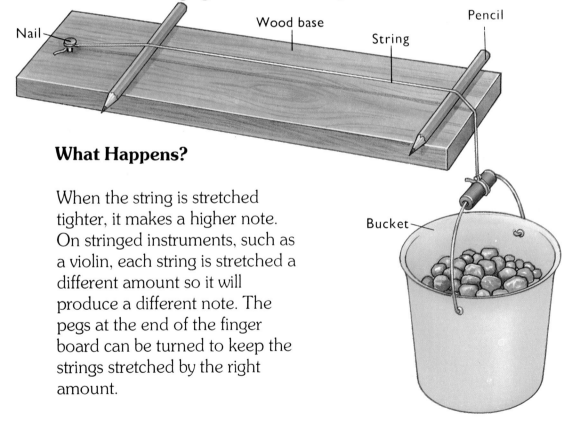

Nail — Wood base   String   Pencil

What Happens?

When the string is stretched tighter, it makes a higher note. On stringed instruments, such as a violin, each string is stretched a different amount so it will produce a different note. The pegs at the end of the finger board can be turned to keep the strings stretched by the right amount.

Bucket —

◄ If you watch someone playing a violin, you will see that they often press the strings down with their fingers. This makes the vibrating part of the string shorter so it makes a higher note.

MAKING MUSIC

In an orchestra, the musicians make air vibrate to produce musical notes in three main ways—with strings, with pipes, or by hitting a surface. The size of the instruments affects the notes they make. Small instruments make high notes and large instruments make low notes.

In the picture, can you find examples of the different kinds of instruments? Look for stringed instruments (such as violin, cello, and piano), woodwind instruments (such as clarinet, flute, and bassoon), brass instruments (such as trumpet, trombone, and french horn) and percussion instruments (such as cymbals, drum, and triangle).

Violin

Trumpet

With Strings

In a stringed instrument, the note depends on the size and length of the string and how tightly it is stretched.

With Pipes

In woodwind and brass instruments, the note depends on the length of the pipe and the materials it is made from.

Drum

By Hitting Things

In percussion instruments, sounds are produced by striking with a special stick or hammer, or by hitting together the instruments themselves. Many of the instruments cannot produce definite notes but some can be tuned.

SOUND MESSAGES

Sounds gives us all sorts of information about our surroundings. The sounds people make tell us when they are happy, sad, angry, or frightened. Some sounds, such as music, are nice to listen to and may help us to relax. Other sounds, such as a police siren, carry an urgent warning message.

▲ Fire engines need to get to a fire as soon as possible. They use a loud bell or a siren to warn other vehicles and people to keep out of their way.

▼ The sound of a bell ringing is very useful for carrying messages. When a telephone rings, we know someone wants to speak to us. When a door bell rings, we know there is someone at the door. When an alarm clock rings, we know it is time to get up. Can you think of any other ways that we use bells to give us information?

Telephone bell

Doorbell

Alarm clock

▲ A rattlesnake makes a loud, buzzing sound by shaking the "rattle" at the end of its tail. This helps to scare off enemies, such as foxes. The rattle is made of old pieces of skin from the tip of the tail. The skin is hard, dry, and hollow. Each time the snake sheds its skin, another piece is added to the rattle.

▶ Frogs make loud calls by moving air to and fro across the vocal cords in the throat. When they push air against the floor of the mouth, it expands like a balloon. The air in the "balloon" vibrates and helps to make the sounds louder. Frogs call to attract a mate and recognize others of their own kind.

TRUE OR FALSE?

1 Sound travels more slowly through solid materials than it does through air.

2 Blowing across a bottle top with a little air inside makes a high note.

3 When a short elastic band is plucked, it produces a lower note than a long elastic band.

4 A sound box makes the notes on a musical instrument louder.

5 A stretched string produces a high note.

6 Frogs make loud calls to attract insects for their supper.

Answers

1 False. Sound travels faster through solid materials than through air. This is because the particles or molecules which make up solids are closer together than they are in air.

2 True. The air vibrates quickly, producing a high note.

3 False. A shorter band vibrates quickly, producing a high note.

4 True. Sound boxes increase the amount of vibrating air, and so make sounds louder.

5 True. Stretched strings vibrate faster than looser ones.

6 False. Frogs call to attract a mate or to recognize others of their own kind.

Air and Flight

Why do you need air to survive? Why do we use baking powder in cooking? Why does a hot-air balloon rise up into the air? How does a barometer work? How does an airplane take off and fly through the air? Why do dandelion seeds have parachutes? Why are birds such efficient flying machines?

This section will help you to discover the answers to these questions and has lots of ideas for ways to investigate air and flight.

In this section, you can discover why we need air to survive, how the weather is caused by moving air, and how machines and animals fly through the air.

The section is divided into six different topics. Look out for the big headings with a circle at each end — like the one at the top of this page.

Air All Around

Air everyday; breathing air.

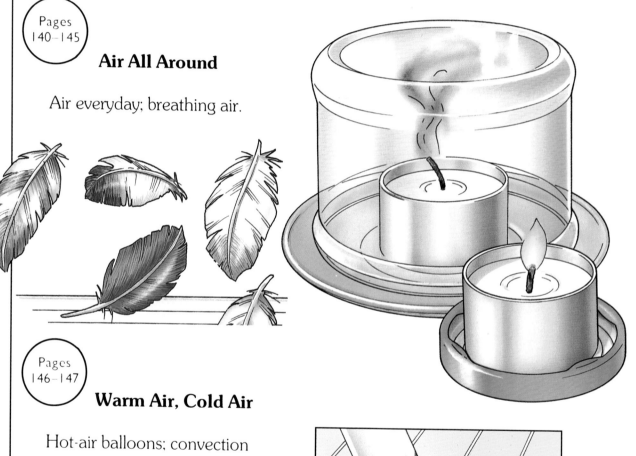

Warm Air, Cold Air

Hot-air balloons; convection currents.

Air Pushes Back

Compressed air; air pressure; siphons.

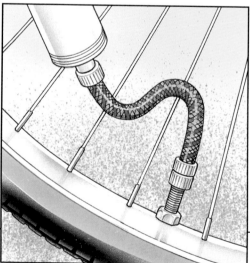

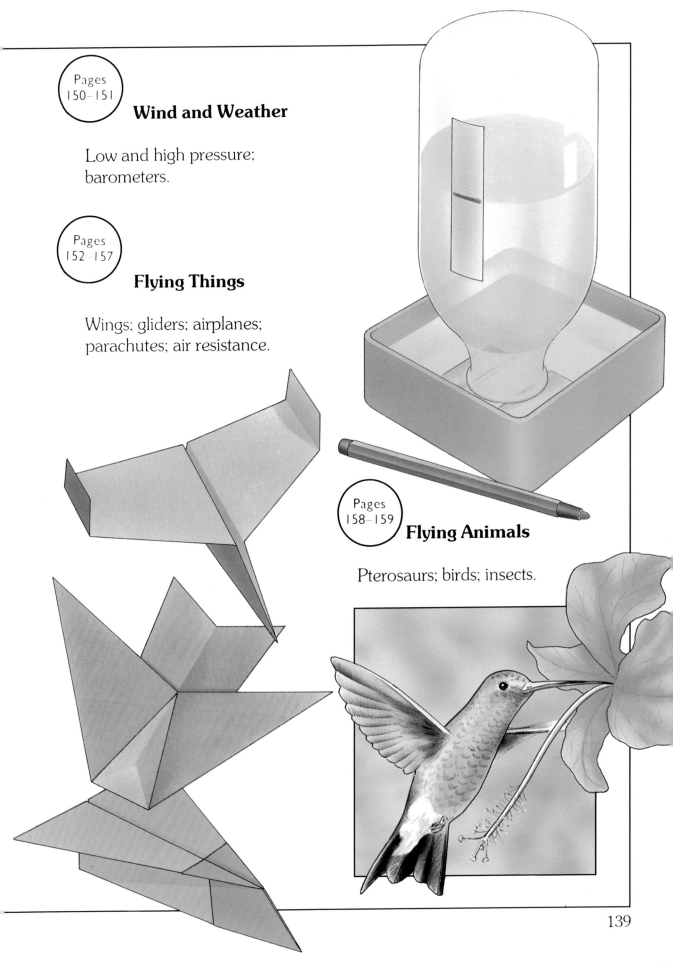

Wind and Weather

Pages
150–151

Low and high pressure;
barometers.

Pages
152–157

Flying Things

Wings; gliders; airplanes;
parachutes; air resistance.

Pages
158–159

Flying Animals

Pterosaurs; birds; insects.

139

Air is everywhere. It fills the space all around you. It is inside plants and animals, bottles and saucepans, bicycle tires and balloons. Soil and water also contain air. Because we cannot see, smell, or taste air, we often forget that it is there. The best way to investigate air is to look at what it does to things around you.

The pictures along the bottom of these two pages will give you some ideas. How many more examples can you think of? Make up a story or write a poem about how air affects your life.

Bubbles of air in a soda drink

▶ When air moves from place to place, we call it the wind. A windy day is a good time to fly a kite. The force of the wind pushes the kite up into the sky.

Blowing up a balloon

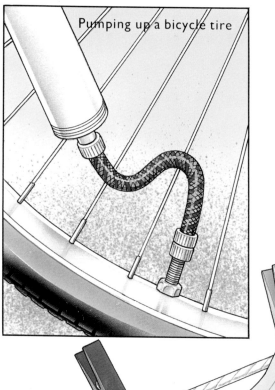

Pumping up a bicycle tire

Rubber ring full of air

Windy weather

Wind drying
the washing

 **Breath Power**

Why do you need air? When you breathe in, air is sucked into your lungs. In your lungs, one of the gases in the air — called oxygen — passes into your blood. The blood carries oxygen to every part of the body. You need oxygen to release the energy stored in your food. Without oxygen, you could not survive. All plants and animals need the oxygen in the air to stay alive.

Count how many times you breathe in during one minute. Then run on the spot or up and down stairs for one minute and count again. Repeat the same test after standing still for five minutes or after cycling or swimming. Compare all your results.

You could also feel your pulse before and after taking exercise. To do this, place a finger on the side of your neck or on the inside of your wrist. Your pulse tells you how fast your heart is beating. When you exercise, you need more oxygen, so you breathe faster. The heart beats faster to pump your blood, and the oxygen it carries, around the body.

How big are your lungs?

You will need:
a large bowl or the bath, a long piece of plastic tubing, masking tape, a large bottle which holds about a gallon of water, a waterproof pen, a measuring jug or cylinder.

This experiment will show the amount of air your lungs hold.

1. Fill the bowl half full of water.
2. Fill the large bottle with water. Stick tape on one side.
3. Hold the bottle over the bowl, put your hand over the neck and carefully turn the bottle upside down. Hold the neck of the bottle under the water. Mark the water level on the tape.
4. Ask a friend to hold the bottle upright and push one end of the plastic tubing into the neck of the bottle.
5. Take a deep breath and blow as hard as you can down the tubing.
6. Mark the level of the water in the bottle when you have finished.
7. Turn the bottle up the right way again. Use the measuring jug or cylinder to pour water into the bottle up to the first mark you made on the side. The amount of water you add is roughly the same as the amount of air in your lungs. It is called your lung capacity.
8. Repeat the test after taking an ordinary breath. How much air do you breathe out this time? Compare your lung capacity with your friends'.

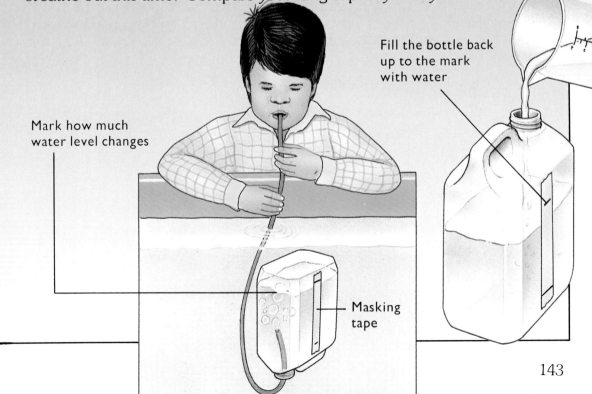

Fill the bottle back up to the mark with water

Mark how much water level changes

Masking tape

143

> **You will need:**
> a small jar, a spoon, a tall bottle, sugar cubes, yeast (fresh or dried), a balloon, string.

Bubbles in Bread

Use the carbon dioxide given off by yeast to blow up a balloon.

Tie the balloon onto the top

1. Half fill a small jar with warm water and add four sugar cubes.
2. Use the spoon to stir the water until the sugar disappears.
3. Pour the sugary water into the tall bottle.
4. Mix one teaspoon of the yeast with a little water.
5. Add this mixture to the bottle.
6. Use the string to tie the balloon over the neck of the bottle. Leave the bottle in a warm place.

Mixture

Yeast

Sugar

What happens

The yeast feeds on the sugar, grows and gives off carbon dioxide gas. This gas will blow up the balloon. It also makes air holes in bread.

Making Cakes

If you make a cake with plain flour, you need to add baking powder to make the cake light and full of air. Baking powder, like yeast, gives off bubbles of carbon dioxide gas if mixed with water and heated.

As Light as Air

You will need:
4 ounces strawberries, 1 packet of strawberry jello, 2 eggs (separated into whites and yolks), 2 ounces caster sugar, 3 ounces cream cheese.
A large bowl, a small bowl, a fork, a spoon, a whisk or a food mixer, a saucepan.

Mousses, meringues, and souffles are light and fluffy because air is whisked into them. Make a strawberry mousse.

1. With an adult, make up the jello following the instructions, but use only 12 fluid ounces of water. Leave the jello in the refrigerator until it starts to thicken.
2. Use the fork to crush the strawberries into a pulp.
3. Ask an adult to help you whisk the egg yolks and sugar in a bowl which is standing in a pan of hot water. The mixture should go thick and pale.
4. Add the crushed stawberries to the egg and sugar mix.
5. When the jello has started to thicken, add a little jello to the cream cheese. Beat the cheese with a spoon. Then add the cheese to the egg mixture, together with the jello.
6. Ask an adult to help you whisk the egg whites until they stand up in stiff peaks.
7. Carefully mix the egg whites into the egg, cheese, and jello mixture.
8. Leave the mousse in the refrigerator until it is set. When you eat the mousse, you will see lots of tiny bubbles of air.

WARM AIR, COLD AIR

Have you ever watched a bonfire? Sparks from the fire are carried upward by warm air rising from the fire. As air gets warmer, the particles of which it is made spread out. This makes the air lighter or less dense so it rises upward. As air cools, it becomes heavier or more dense and sinks downward again. When heat is carried by the air itself, the process is called convection.

Falling feathers

Let go of a small feather in different places around a room. Can you find any places where the feather will rise? (A warm radiator is a good place to try.) How high does the feather rise? How long is it in the air?

Bubbles, talcum powder, or flour will also help you to detect rising hot air currents.

▲ Air inside a hot-air balloon is heated by a gas flame below the balloon. The hot air inside the balloon is lighter or less dense than the cooler air outside the balloon. As the hot air rises, it carries the balloon upward. When the gas flame is turned down, the air cools and the balloon sinks back to the ground.

Can you use a balloon to lift up a plastic beaker? Put the balloon inside the beaker and blow up the balloon. You will find that the sides of the balloon grip the beaker tightly. You should be able to lift up the beaker just by holding on to the neck of the balloon.

This works because air can be squeezed or compressed into a smaller space. The compressed air inside the balloon presses outward on the sides of the beaker, so you can lift it up. Air pressure can be a powerful force.

The air around presses against us equally in all directions. The pressure of the air in any place is caused by the weight of all the air pressing down on that place. Things have weight because gravity pulls them to the ground. This test shows that air has weight.

Tie a piece of string to the middle of a thin stick and hang the string from a hook. Blow up two identical balloons, making one bigger than the other. Tie one balloon on to each end of the stick. The end with the bigger balloon will dip down. It is heavier than the smaller balloon because it contains more air.

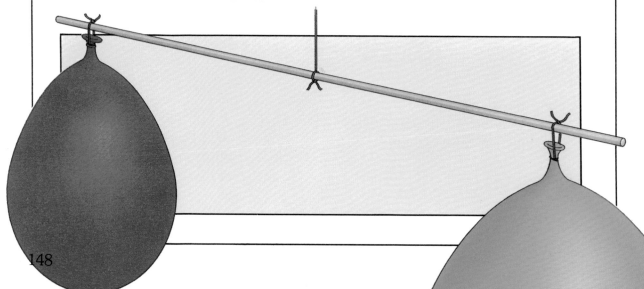

Upside-down Water

Hold a glass over a sink or a bowl and fill it right to the top with water. Carefully slide a smooth piece of card, such as a postcard, over the top. Hold your hand on the card and slowly turn the glass upside down. When you take away your hand, what happens?

What happens
The air pushes against the card and should keep the water in the glass. The pressure of the air upward is greater than the pressure of the water downward.

Make a Siphon

1. Fill two large jars with water. Hold some plastic tubing under water in a bowl until the air has escaped.
2. Pinch both tube ends and put one end under water in each jar. Lift one jar up and down.

What happens
When one jar is lower than the other, the air pressing down on the water in the top jar will force the water up the tube, and down into the other jar.

Weather is produced by air moving from place to place — which we call winds. Winds are caused by warm air rising and cooler air moving in to take its place. Warm air is lighter or less dense than cool air, so it creates low air pressure. Cool air is heavier or more dense and creates high air pressure. Usually we have fine weather when the air pressure is high. Low air pressure brings clouds, rain, or snow.

▼ Winds can sometimes blow at tremendous speeds and cause great damage. The winds produced by a hurricane can travel at 180 miles an hour. This picture shows the damage from a hurricane in Darwin, Australia.

Make a Barometer

A barometer measures air pressure. A change in the air pressure tells us when the weather is likely to change.

You will need:
a tall, clear bottle, a saucer or dish, two thin pieces of wood, tape, a pen.

1. Fill the bottle with water. Hold the saucer or dish over the top of the bottle and carefully turn the bottle upside down. Some of the water will spill out, so do this over a sink or a bowl.
2. Stand the saucer or dish with the bottle inside it in a cool place.
3. Tilt the bottle to let some air in. It needs to be about one-third full of air.
4. Slip the pieces of wood under the bottle to lift it clear of the saucer or dish. This lets water move in and out of the bottle.
5. Stick a long piece of tape on the side of the bottle and mark the level of the water.
6. Watch your barometer carefully and mark the level of the water at regular intervals. Can you predict the weather with your barometer?

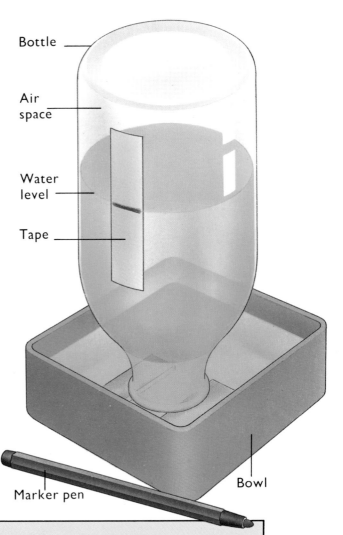

Bottle

Air space

Water level

Tape

Marker pen

Bowl

What happens
When the air pressure increases, it pushes down on the water in the dish, forcing the water up the bottle. When the air pressure falls, the level of water in the bottle falls too. Better weather will usually follow when the barometer rises and worse weather when it falls.

FLYING THINGS

How many flying things can you think of? Some flying things are alive. They are animals or parts of plants. Others are machines made by people.

You could make a scrapbook of flying things. Fill your scrapbook with drawings, postcards, and pictures cut out of newspapers or magazines.

Can you make a piece of paper fly through the air? First, drop the paper from a height. As the sheet of paper falls, air is trapped underneath. As the air escapes, it makes the paper sway.

Fold the paper in half and open it out. Fold one of the long edges back. Drop the paper from a height again.

The center fold makes the air pressure the same on both sides of the paper and this stops it rolling from side to side. Folding a long edge makes one side of the paper heavier, so the paper pushes through air more easily.

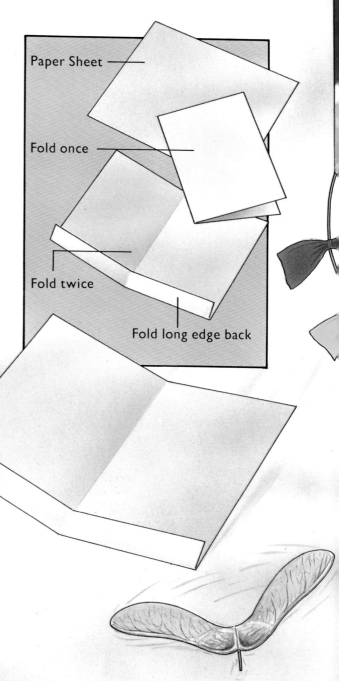

Paper Sheet

Fold once

Fold twice

Fold long edge back

▲ Have you ever seen people hang gliding? As the wings of the glider move through the air, they help to lift the glider upward. Warm air currents rising up from the ground also help to push the glider up into the sky.

153

▲ To take off, a plane uses its engines to move fast along the runway. As it moves, air flows above and below the wings and produces lift. When there is enough lift to overcome the force of gravity, the plane takes off. In the air, the plane is slowed down by the resistance or drag of the air. The power of the engines has to overcome this dragging effect to keep the plane moving.

 **Making an Airplane**

> **You will need:**
> a straw, paperclips, stiff paper, a pencil, tape, scissors.

1. Make a wing shape, with the top edge curved, from a piece of stiff paper about 9 inches by 5 inches.
2. Tape the back edge of the wing and cut ailerons in this edge.
3. For the tail, cut a piece of stiff paper about 8 inches by $1\frac{1}{2}$ inches and fold the middle so it sticks up. Cut away about half an inch of the flat pieces either side of the tail.
4. Cut elevators in the flat edges of the tail piece.
5. Use tape to fix the wings and tail piece to the straw.
6. Weight the nose of the plane with several paperclips.

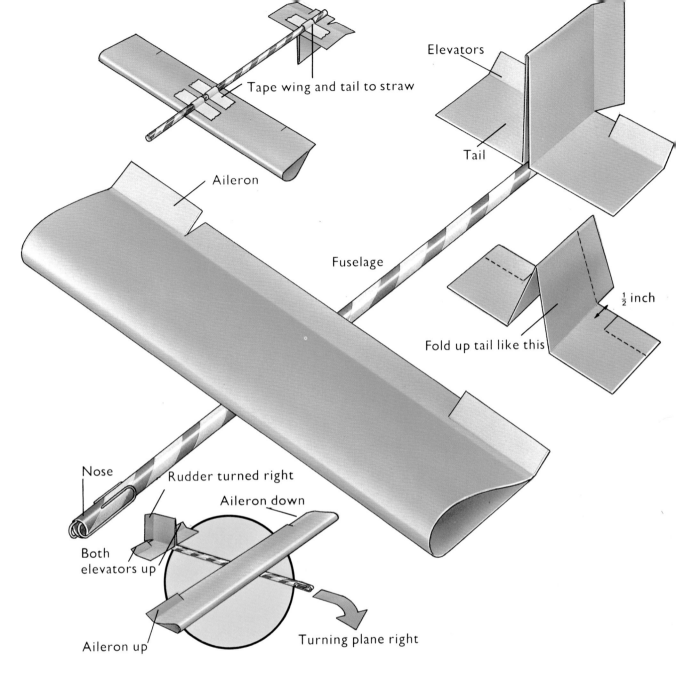

Tape wing and tail to straw

Elevators

Tail

Aileron

Fuselage

½ inch

Fold up tail like this

Nose

Rudder turned right

Aileron down

Both
elevators up

Aileron up

Turning plane right

7. Now bend the flaps up and down and the rudder from side to side to see how this affects the flight of the plane.

Have you ever noticed the flaps on the wings and tail piece of a passenger airplane? The flaps on the wings are called ailerons. The ones on the tail piece are called elevators. The pilot moves the ailerons and elevators, together with a tail flap called the rudder, to make the plane turn, climb, or dive through the air. Make your own plane to see how this works.

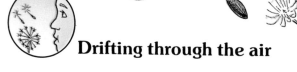

Drifting through the air

Air resistance can sometimes be useful if we want to slow flying things down. For instance, parachutes slow down things falling down to the ground. A dandelion seed has a little parachute to help it drift slowly on the wind. This helps it to cover long distances and to move away from its parent plant.

Make Parachutes

You will need:
scissors, thread or string, different materials and loads.

1. Cut some squares out of different materials. Make the squares different sizes.
2. Use tape to fix thread or string to each corner of the squares.
3. Tie a load to the strings under each parachute, and launch it.
4. How long does each parachute take to fall down to the ground? Do larger parachutes fall more quickly or more slowly? If the parachute is carrying a heavy load, does this make a difference?
5. Make a small hole in the top of one of the parachutes. How does this affect the way it falls down?

What happens

The force of gravity pulls the parachute down to the ground. But some air is trapped under the parachute. This air gets squashed, pushes up against the parachute and makes it fall more slowly.

▲ Modern parachutes have a hole in the top. This helps the air trapped inside the parachute to escape more smoothly and stops the parachute from wobbling and swaying as it falls through the air.

▶ Some animals, such as this colugo, have flaps of skin along the sides of the body. When they spread out this skin, they can glide through the air like living parachutes. The colugo can glide as far as 400 feet between trees.

157

The first flying animals on Earth were probably insects. About 200 million years ago, winged reptiles called pterosaurs flew in the skies above the dinosaurs. The wings of pterosaurs were made of skin stretched between their arms and legs, rather like the wings of the bats alive today. The largest pterosaurs had wings that were as big as a small airplane.

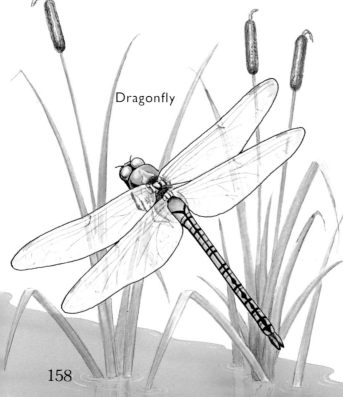

Dragonfly

Nowadays, only birds, bats, and insects have wings to power flight upward instead of just gliding along. Being able to fly is very useful. It helps animals to escape from danger as well as find food and places to nest.

Insects have very thin, flat wings with powerful muscles. As they flap their wings, they push against the air and this makes them move upward and forward. Flies can beat their wings as fast as 1,000 times a second.

▲ As a bird's wings beat downward, they create more air pressure under the wings. This extra pressure pushes the bird upward. When the wings are pulled up again, the tips of the feathers move apart to let air flow through.

▼ Hummingbirds are like tiny helicopters. They can fly sideways, backward and even upside-down. Hummingbirds beat their wings between 22 and 78 times a second and can fly up to 40 miles per hour.

Birds are well designed living flying machines. Their body is light in weight and some of their bones are hollow to reduce weight. Their feathers fit closely together to give them a smooth, streamlined shape. And their front arms have become wings. A bird's wing is shaped like an airfoil to give it lift. Birds have very powerful chest muscles to beat their wings up and down.

TRUE OR FALSE?

3 Air cannot be squashed into a small space.

1 Meringues are light because of all the air whisked into them.

2 Cold air is lighter or less dense than warm air.

6 Bats have feathers on their wings.

4 Low air pressure usually brings bad weather.

5 Flaps on the wings and tail of airplanes help them to climb, turn, and dive.

Answers

1 True. All the bubbles of air make meringues light and fluffy.

2 False. Cold air is heavier or more dense than warm air, which will rise.

3 False. Air can be squashed or compressed into small spaces. Bicycle tires are pumped full of compressed air.

4 True. With low air pressure, air rises and cools to form clouds.

5 True. The flaps control the way air flows over the wings. They allow the pilot to change the position of the aircraft.

6 False. The wings of a bat are made of skin.

Color and Light

Can monkeys see in color? What are the primary colors of paint? How can you make colored dyes from plants? Which kitchen chemicals are acids or alkalis? Which colors make up a television picture? How many colors are there in a rainbow? How do color filters work?

This section will help you to discover the answers to these questions and has lots of ideas for ways to investigate color and light.

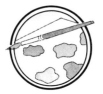 

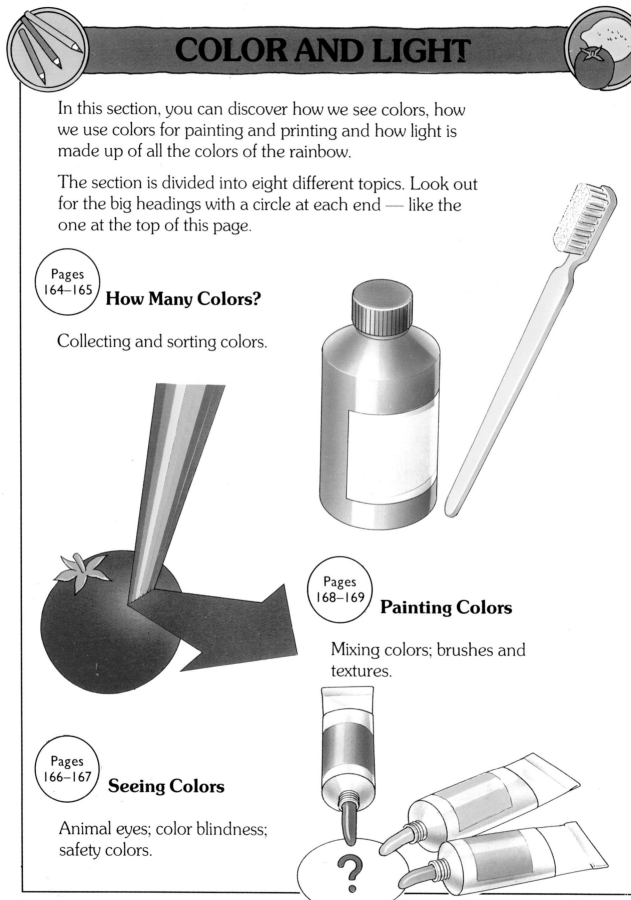

COLOR AND LIGHT

In this section, you can discover how we see colors, how we use colors for painting and printing and how light is made up of all the colors of the rainbow.

The section is divided into eight different topics. Look out for the big headings with a circle at each end — like the one at the top of this page.

Pages 164–165

How Many Colors?

Collecting and sorting colors.

Pages 168–169

Painting Colors

Mixing colors; brushes and textures.

Pages 166–167

Seeing Colors

Animal eyes; color blindness; safety colors.

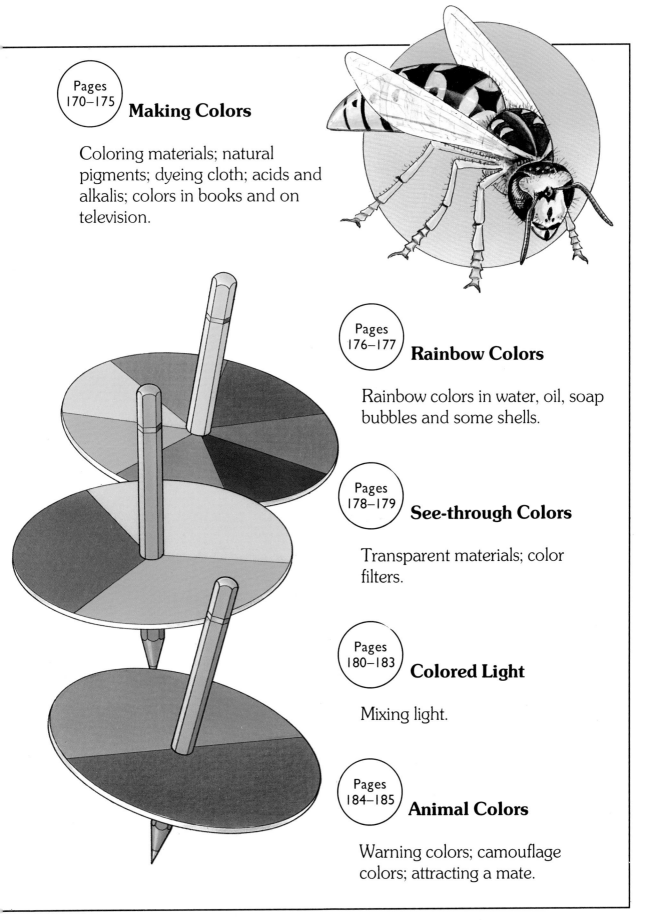

HOW MANY COLORS?

Make a collection of different colored objects like the ones along the edges of these two pages. Look for some natural materials as well as artificial ones. Sort your collection into sets such as happy and sad colors or summer and winter colors. How many different shades of the same color can you find?

Another way of sorting your collection would be to put all the things made from the same material (such as paper, plastic, or cloth) together.

▶ How many different colors can you find in the picture? What is your favorite color?

We see things because light bounces off objects into our eyes. This "bouncing off" effect is called reflection. The light from the Sun or an electric light bulb looks white, but it is really made up of all the colors of the rainbow. The colors we see depend on the colors that are reflected off objects into our eyes. For instance, a tomato looks red because it reflects red light and absorbs the other colors.

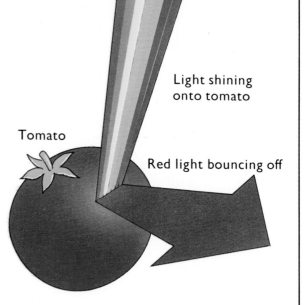

Light shining onto tomato

Tomato

Red light bouncing off

If an object absorbs all the rainbow colors in light, no light is reflected and we see black. If an object reflects all the colors, we see white.

Animal Eyesight

Did you know that many animals, such as cats, dogs, horses, and cows, cannot see the colors we see? Their world is full of shades of black and white and gray. Apes and monkeys, however, seem to be able to see the same colors that we can and some animals, especially birds, may have better color vision than we do. Animals that are brightly colored can nearly always see colors.

Your view

Dog's view

Eye Colors

We see colors because of special cells that make up part of the lining of the eyeball. These cells are cone-shaped, so they are called cones. In each eye, there are about 7 million cones. One type of cone responds to red light, a second type responds to green light, and a third type responds to blue light. The cones send messages to the brain and, by joining together the messages it receives, the brain tells us what colors we are seeing.

This test shows you more about how you see colors. Draw a red shape on a piece of white paper. Stare hard at your drawing for a minute. Then stare at a blank piece of white paper. What color is your drawing now? Repeat the test with a blue object.

What happens

The cones that respond to red light quickly get tired so they stop working for a while. When you stare at the white paper, only the green and blue cones are working. So you see a greeny-blue picture. This color is called cyan. With the blue object, only the red and green cones are working, so you see yellow.

Color Blindness

Some people are color blind, which means they cannot tell the difference between certain colors. Very few people are truly color blind and see only black, white and gray.

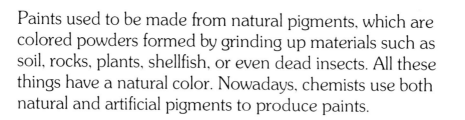

PAINTING COLORS

Paints used to be made from natural pigments, which are colored powders formed by grinding up materials such as soil, rocks, plants, shellfish, or even dead insects. All these things have a natural color. Nowadays, chemists use both natural and artificial pigments to produce paints.

Mixing Paints

Most colors of paint can be made by mixing together red, yellow, and blue paint. These are called the primary colors of paint. The colors we see are the colors reflected by the paints. Yellow paint mixed with red paint gives an orange color because orange is the only color reflected by both paints. What colors do you get by mixing blue and yellow paint or green and red paint?

If you mix red, yellow, and blue paint of exactly the right shades and brightness, you should make black. In fact, you are more likely to get a muddy brown.

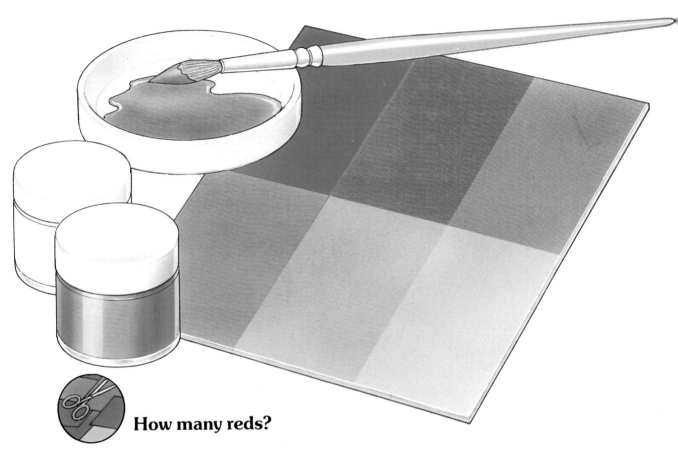

How many reds?

Have you ever looked at the paint charts in do-it-yourself stores? You can buy lots of different shades of one color and it is often hard to choose the right one for your room.

See if you can mix up six shades of one color, such as red. Divide up a piece of paper into six equal sized strips. Put bright red in the first strip and then keep adding white paint, a little at a time, to make lighter reds. When the paint is dry, write a number on the back of each strip. Make one the deepest color and six the palest color. Then cut up all the squares and mix them up. Can you sort them back into the right order?

MAKING COLORS

As well as paints, there are several other coloring materials, such as wax crayons, coloring pencils, chalk, charcoal, ink, and felt pens. Draw an outline shape several times and color each one in with a different coloring material. How do they look different? Which coloring material is easiest to use? Which do you like best? What happens if you put the coloring materials on a wet surface? Do they mix with water?

▼ Stone Age artists painted the walls of these caves between 12,000 and 30,000 years ago. They mixed up their colors from natural pigments in the soil, rocks, or minerals. They ground up these pigments into a smooth paste with simple tools called pestles and mortars, and mixed the colors together on the stones. They probably added some animal fat to make the colors waterproof. The artists used brushes made of animal hair, chewed twigs, and pads of moss and fur. All their paintings were done using only the flickering light from small lamps which burned animal fat.

Making yellow dye

You will need:
2 ounces of alum, 1 tablespoon of cream of tartar, an ounce of onion skins, cloth, a sieve, 2 large saucepans, a jar.

You can use the colored juices from plants to dye cloth or wool. Some dyes do not give permanent colors unless another chemical is added. These chemicals are called mordants. They "fix" the color by making it bite into the cloth so the colors last. In the past, tree bark and wood ash have been used as mordants. Nowadays, you can buy artificial mordants from the chemist.

1. Mix the alum and cream of tartar with 20 fluid ounces of warm water in the jar. Add to a large pan of cold water.
2. Put the cloth in the pan and ask an adult to help you heat it gradually. Stir until it boils.
3. Simmer gently for about an hour, then leave to cool down.
4. Take out the cloth and leave it in a plastic bag.
5. Ask an adult to help you boil the onion skins in a deep pan full of water and simmer for an hour.
6. Strain the liquid through a sieve to get rid of the skins.
7. Put your damp cloth into the pan and boil up the water again. Simmer gently for one hour.
8. Switch off the heat and leave the pan to cool.
9. Take the cloth out of the pan and rinse it thoroughly.
10. Leave the cloth to dry.

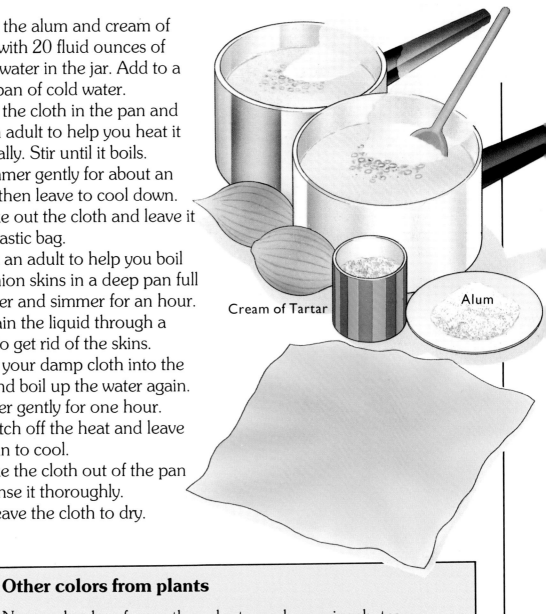

Cream of Tartar

Alum

Other colors from plants

Now make dyes from other plants, such as spinach, tea leaves, red cabbage, pine cones, and blackberries. You can also dye wool instead of cloth.

Kitchen Chemicals

You can use a solution of colored dye to find out if the chemicals in the kitchen are acids or alkalis. Acids and alkalis are chemical opposites. They behave differently when they are mixed with other chemicals. A dye that changes color when it is mixed with acids or alkalis is called an indicator. You can make an indicator from red cabbage.

1. Chop up some red cabbage leaves and put them in a bowl.
2. Add a little sand and mash up the leaves with the back of an old spoon. The sand helps to break up the cabbage leaves so the dye can get out.
3. Ask an adult to add some very hot water to the bowl. Leave the cabbage to soak until cool.
4. Pour the liquid through a sieve to get rid of the cabbage leaves. You will be left with a colored indicator solution. Put this into a bottle or jar with a lid.
5. In a saucer or a jar, mix a small amount of the indicator solution with some of the different chemicals in the kitchen. Good things to try are lemon juice, baking powder, vinegar, washing powder, and soapy water.

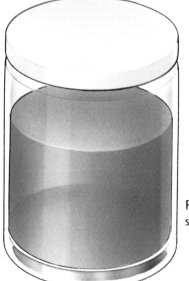

Put dye in screw top jar

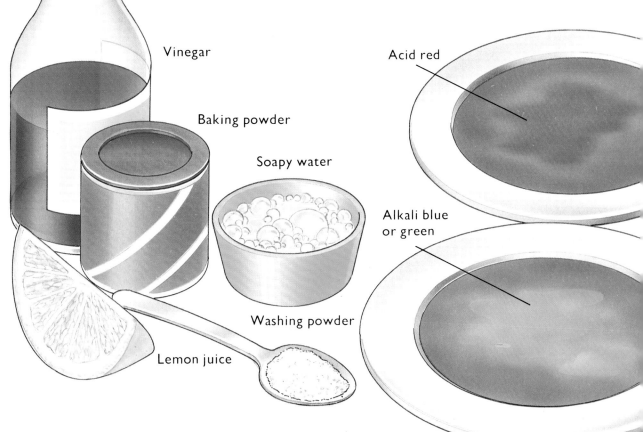

Vinegar

Baking powder

Soapy water

Acid red

Alkali blue
or green

Washing powder

Lemon juice

What happens

If acidic chemicals are mixed with the indicator solution, it will turn red or orange. If the chemicals are alkaline, the solution will turn blue or green. How many acids and alkalis can you find?

Did You Know?

The poison in a bee sting is an acid and the poison in a wasp sting is an alkali.

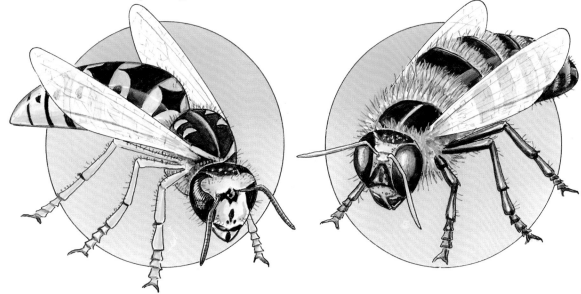

Lots of Dots

Use a magnifying glass to look closely at the pictures in a newspaper. You will see that each one is made up of lots of black dots. The dots are largest in the dark areas and very small in the pale areas. The pale areas look gray, even though only black ink is used.

Book Colors

The color pictures in a book are also made up of lots of dots. The original picture is broken down into four colors — the primary pigments red, blue, and yellow, plus black. The black helps to add in fine detail and make some areas darker.

Each color is printed as tiny dots. Because the dots are so small, our eyes can't see them — unless we use a magnifying glass. So we see areas of flat color, which look like the original colors of the picture. If the dots are not printed in exactly the right place, the picture looks fuzzy.

Blue is a blue-green color called cyan

Dotty television

The colors of a television picture are also made up of a pattern of tiny colored dots of light. From a distance, these dots merge together to make a many-colored picture and we are not aware of the dots. A television picture is made up of red, blue, and green dots because these are the primary colors of light. They are different from the primary colors of paint.

Red is a pinky-red color called magenta

Yellow is just yellow

Black is just black

▲ Have you ever seen a rainbow on a sunny day when it is raining? Rainbows sometimes appear in the spray of water from a waterfall too. The raindrops or water drops make the light spread out so we can see the different colors. Some people think they can see the seven different colors in a rainbow — red, orange, yellow, green, blue, indigo, and violet. How many colors can you see in a rainbow?

Where have you seen rainbow colors? Take a bowl of water out into some bright sunshine. Put a few drops of oil on the surface of the water. How many colors can you see? What happens if you add more water or more oil? If you stir the water with a stick, do the colors change?

Soap bubbles also have rainbow colors in them. Do big bubbles have different color patterns from small bubbles? Do the colors in a bubble change in sunlight?

Oil on water

Soap bubbles

Abalone shell

If you look at some shells, such as this abalone shell, you will also see rainbow colors.

The colors in oil, soap bubbles and some shells are caused by the way light is reflected between the thin outer layers of each object. The rainbow colors are not spread out as they are in a real rainbow.

177

SEE-THROUGH COLORS

Some materials, such as clear glass, plexiglas, and water will let light pass through them. They are said to be transparent. If you look through transparent materials, they change the colors of the things you see.

Make a collection of transparent materials, such as colored bottles, candy wrappings, and plastic. You could also color the water in a clear bottle with ink or food coloring. How do these materials change the color of things you see through them? Is there any difference if you overlap two colors?

What happens

The transparent materials are all types of filter. They let light of the same color pass through but they stop other colors getting through. For instance, a red filter lets red light through, but stops the other colors.

▲ If you look at the light coming through a stained glass window, it will be the same colors as the glass itself. Each piece of glass only lets through light of the same color as itself.

COLORED LIGHT

Mixing colored light does not give the same results as mixing colored paints. This investigation shows how it is different.

You will need:
three flashlights, pieces of red, blue, and green cellophane, tape, white card.

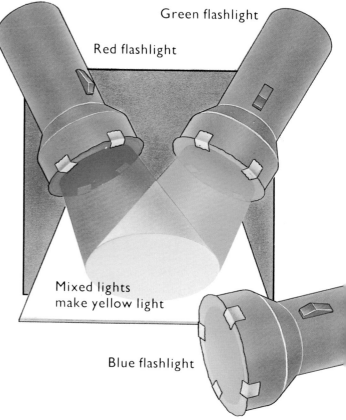

Green flashlight

Red flashlight

Mixed lights make yellow light

Blue flashlight

1. Cut pieces of cellophane which are the right size to fit over the front of the flashlights. Make one torch red, one torch blue, and one torch green.
2. In a darkened room, shine the red and green flashlights onto the white card. Where the beams of light meet on the card, you should see yellow light.
3. Try mixing blue and green light or blue and red light. What colors do they make?
4. Now try mixing all three colors. What happens this time?

What happens

All the colors of the rainbow can be made by mixing the primary colors of light, which are red, blue, and green. Can you remember the primary colors of paint? The colors you make by mixing the primary colors of either light or paint are called secondary colors. Yellow is one secondary color of light. The others are dark pink (magenta) and green-blue (cyan). By mixing all three primary colors of light, you make white light.

▲ Colored lights are often mixed together in different ways to change the atmosphere and create special effects at concerts. Color filters are put in front of white spotlights to light up the stage and make the different colors.

The colors of animals help them to survive in many different ways. They may help them to hide or to attract a mate. Some animals can even change color if their surroundings change.

Warning Colors

Some animals are poisonous or have a nasty sting. These animals are often brightly colored to warn other animals to leave them alone.

Milkweed butterfly caterpillars pick up their poisons by eating the leaves of the Milkweed plants. These poisons are passed on to the adults when the caterpillar changes into a butterfly. Many stinging insects, such as wasps and bees, have black and yellow warning colors.

Colorful Males

Male birds of paradise have colorful, spectacular feathers which they show off in a special display to attract a mate. Sometimes they even hang upside down from the tree branches and wave their feathers up and down. The female birds are fairly plain colors and this helps to hide them from enemies when they are sitting on the eggs.

▲ Chameleons can change their colors by changing the size of spots of pigments in the skin. Their colors often match the colors of the trees and bushes they live in and this helps to camouflage them.

Winter Colors

Some animals such as the snow shoe hare live in places where it snows in winter. They grow a white winter coat which helps them to blend into a snowy background. In spring, they grow a darker colored coat again.

TRUE OR FALSE?

1 If an object reflects all the colors in light, we see white.

2 Dogs can see in color.

3 Acids turn indicator solutions red.

4 A color filter stops light of the same color getting through.

5 Mixing red and green light gives yellow light.

6 Chameleons turn white in winter.

Answers

1 True. If an object absorbs all the colors in light, we see black.

2 False. Dogs, cats, horses and cows cannot see in color, but birds and monkeys can.

3 True. Alkalis turn indicator solutions blue or green.

4 False. A color filter lets light of the **same** color pass through.

5 True. Mixing light is different from mixing paint.

6 False. Chameleons can change color to match their background, but do not live in snowy places, so do not need to turn white.

184

Growing Plants

How can you grow new potatoes from old ones? How much water do seeds need to grow? How can you tell the age of a twig? Why do some kinds of lichen find it hard to grow in polluted air? How can you sort out different kinds of soil?

This section will help you to discover the answers to these questions and has lots of ideas for ways to investigate growing plants.

GROWING PLANTS

In this section, you can discover how to grow plants from cuttings, seeds, and bulbs and how the environment affects plant growth.

The book is divided into five different topics. Look out for the big headings with a circle at each end — like the one at the top of this page.

Pages 188–191

Growing New Plants

Bulbs and tubers.

Pages 192–194

Water, Light, Air, Warmth

Seeds and water; roots and water.

Have you ever grown a carrot top? If you put the top of a carrot in a saucer of water, it will sprout leaves. The leaves use the food stored in the carrot to grow. How long does it take for the leaves to appear?

You could also grow tops of other fruits or vegetables, such as pineapples, parsnips, or turnips. How are they different from the carrot?

Pineapple top

▼ How many different kinds of bulb flowers can you see in this picture? As each new bulb is exactly the same as its parent, people can grow lots of bulbs that are exactly the same.

Seeds, Bulbs, and Cuttings

There are lots of different ways to grow plants. Here are the three main ways.

We can grow some new plants from seeds, which are produced in flowers. Each seed may grow into a new plant that is different from its parent plant.

Seeds

Some plants grow long, spindly stems and sprout new plants at intervals along the stem. These new plants are identical to their parent plants.

Runner

Other new plants grow from pieces of old plants, such as bulbs or cuttings of stems or leaves. These new plants are also identical to their parent plants.

Bulb

Cutting

189

Looking Inside Bulbs

A bulb is an underground stem. It is made up of a flattened stem and a bud surrounded by short swollen leaves. The leaves are full of stored food. In winter, leaves above the ground turn brown and die. Next spring new leaves grow using the food stored in the bulb.

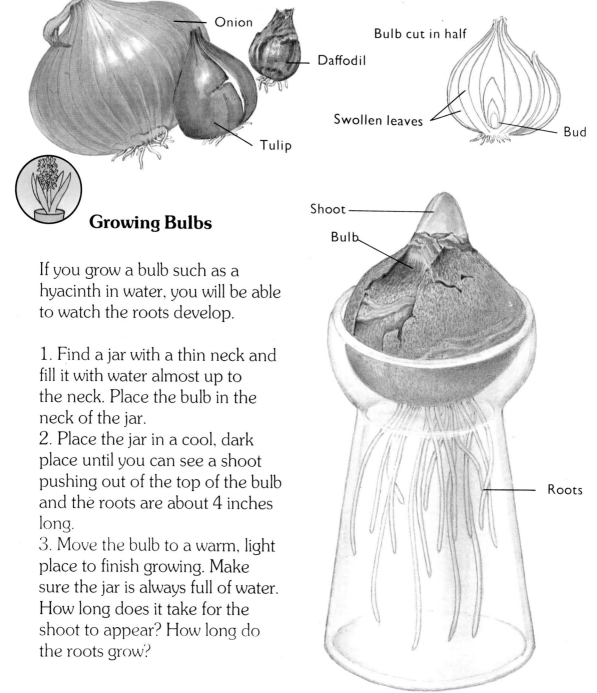

Onion

Daffodil

Bulb cut in half

Tulip

Swollen leaves

Bud

Shoot

Bulb

Roots

Growing Bulbs

If you grow a bulb such as a hyacinth in water, you will be able to watch the roots develop.

1. Find a jar with a thin neck and fill it with water almost up to the neck. Place the bulb in the neck of the jar.
2. Place the jar in a cool, dark place until you can see a shoot pushing out of the top of the bulb and the roots are about 4 inches long.
3. Move the bulb to a warm, light place to finish growing. Make sure the jar is always full of water. How long does it take for the shoot to appear? How long do the roots grow?

Potting Potatoes

Like bulbs, potatoes are a kind of underground stem. They are called tubers. Tubers store food both to produce new plants and to help the plant survive underground when conditions are not good for growing. The "eyes" of a potato are really buds, which will sprout into shoots and grow leaves. You can grow several new plants from one potato.

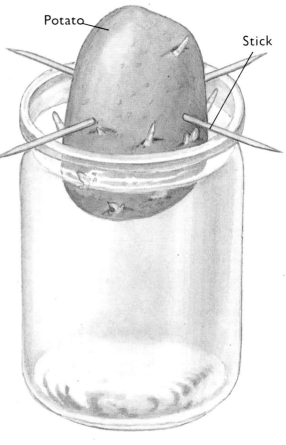

Potato

Stick

1. Push four sticks into one end of a potato.
2. Balance the potato over a glass jar full of water. Keep the jar topped up with water.
3. In a few days, shoots will grow from the eyes. Take the potato out of the water and ask an adult to help you cut out each shoot, with a little piece of potato behind it.
4. Plant each shoot in a separate plant pot, covering with soil or potting compost.

191

WATER, LIGHT, AIR, WARMTH

How does the environment around a plant affect the way it grows? Four of the most important factors are water, light, air, and temperature. To investigate water, make four equal groups of cress seeds and soak three overnight.

 **Plants and Water**

1. In the first container, put some wet seeds on wet absorbent cotton.
2. In the second container, put wet seeds on dry cotton.
3. In the third container, put another group of wet seeds on top of dry cotton. Cover the seeds and cotton with water. Keep these seeds and those in the first container damp.
4. In the last container, put the dry seeds on top of dry cotton. Cover all containers and leave for a few days.

What happens

Seeds need the right amount of water to germinate properly. Dry seeds on dry cotton will not grow at all. Wet seeds on dry cotton will shrivel up and die. Seeds under water will go rotten. Only wet seeds on wet cotton grow well.

Make a clown from modeling clay, leaving a dip in its head. Put damp cress seeds on damp cotton in the dip. Watch the clown's hair grow.

Roots and Water

1. Place a clay flower pot full of water in a large bowl.
2. Pack a mixture of soil and sawdust around the pot.
3. Put some soaked peas on the surface of the soil.
4. After a few days, brush the soil off the peas. In which direction are the roots growing?

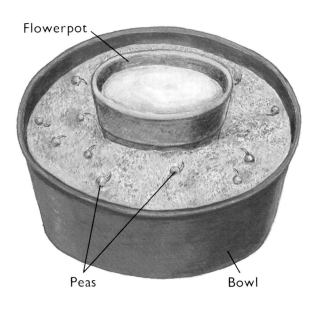

Flowerpot

Peas

Bowl

What happens

When the only source of water is in the flower pot, the roots grow sideways toward the water. Water is so important to the seeds that the need for water overcomes the pull of gravity.

▼ Rice is planted in fields which are flooded with water. These are called paddy fields. Rice grows well with its roots in lots of water and its shoots in the air.

Airy Plants

Air is very important to plants. Can you think why we put water weeds in a fish tank?

Cut a short length of pondweed and leave it in a jar on a sunny windowsill. Look carefully at the leaves. Can you see any bubbles in the water? When plants make food, they also give off a gas called oxygen. The bubbles given off by the pondweed are bubbles of oxygen. This is the gas that plants and animals, including fishes, need to breathe to stay alive.

Air bubbles

Hot and Cold Plants

Keep two similar seedlings at different temperatures to see how this affects their growth. Put one in a warm place and one in a cold place. Make sure both seedlings have the same amount of light so they can make food.

Some seeds, such as apple seeds, need a cold period before they will sprout. In the natural world, this means seeds shed in autumn will not grow until warmer weather returns in spring.

Put apple seeds in the refrigerator for a few days before planting.

In a cool place

In a hot place

SORTING OUT SOILS

Plants need water and minerals from the soil in order to grow well. There are lots of different kinds of soil, such as clay soil, sandy soil, or chalky soil. Some plants only grow well in certain types of soil.

Clay soils hold water and often become waterlogged. In sandy soils, water quickly drains away. In winter, the water in the soil is frozen. Trees with wide, flat leaves cannot draw up enough water to replace that lost from their leaves. So they drop their leaves and rest over the winter.

Collect some soils and see how many differences you can find. What is the texture like? Is the soil smooth, sticky, or gritty? Look at the soil carefully with a magnifying glass.

Separating Soil

Make the soil separate by shaking some up in a jar of water and leaving it to soak for a day or two. How many layers can you see? How big are the pieces on the bottom? Are there any bits floating on the surface? Try this investigation again with different kinds of soil.

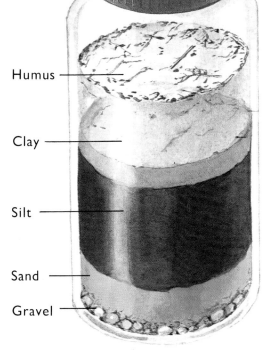

Humus

Clay

Silt

Sand

Gravel

HOW TREES GROW

Trees grow in two main ways. The twigs and branches grow longer at the tips, so the tree becomes taller and wider. At the same time, the trunk, branches, and twigs all grow fatter. Twigs form new buds at the end of the year.

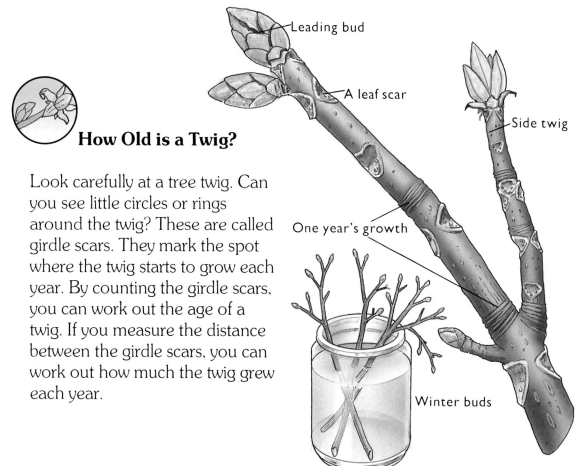

Leading bud

A leaf scar

Side twig

One year's growth

Winter buds

How Old is a Twig?

Look carefully at a tree twig. Can you see little circles or rings around the twig? These are called girdle scars. They mark the spot where the twig starts to grow each year. By counting the girdle scars, you can work out the age of a twig. If you measure the distance between the girdle scars, you can work out how much the twig grew each year.

Growing Buds

The winter buds on a tree contain the beginnings of the shoot, leaves, and flowers for the following year. The thick, overlapping scales protect the delicate contents of the bud from cold, from insect attack, or from drying out. In spring, bring some twigs indoors and leave them in a jar of water in a warm, sunny place. The best trees to try are horse chestnut, willow, or birch. The buds may take some weeks to open, but you can watch how the leaves unfold and burst out of the scales.

Trees from Twigs

You can grow trees from small pieces of twig. It is better to pull off the twig, rather than cutting it. Take a small piece of the main twig too. Plant the twig upright in soil or potting compost or leave it in a jar of water until it has grown some roots, and then plant it. Try this with willow, poplar, or hawthorn trees.

How Tall is a Tree?

Here is a simple way to measure how high a tree has grown. Hold a stick or a pencil in front of you, and walk backward and forward until the top and bottom of the stick or pencil are level with the top and bottom of the tree. Turn the pencil on its side and ask a friend to walk away from the tree at right angles to you. Stop them when he or she is level with the end of the pencil. You can then measure the distance between the tree and your friend. This distance will equal the height of the tree.

Did You Know?

The largest living thing on Earth is the General Sherman Sequoi Tree in California. It is 275 feet tall, and the trunk weighs approximately 1,200 tons. Experts believe that this giant tree is over 2,500 years old.

▲ Bonsai trees start off as normal trees but do not get enough food and water to grow to their normal size. They are miniatures, and their shoots and roots are pruned to stunt their growth. Bonsai trees can take hundreds of years to grow. If you keep trimming the leaves and shoots of a tree seedling, giving it only a little room to grow, you can make your own bonsai tree.

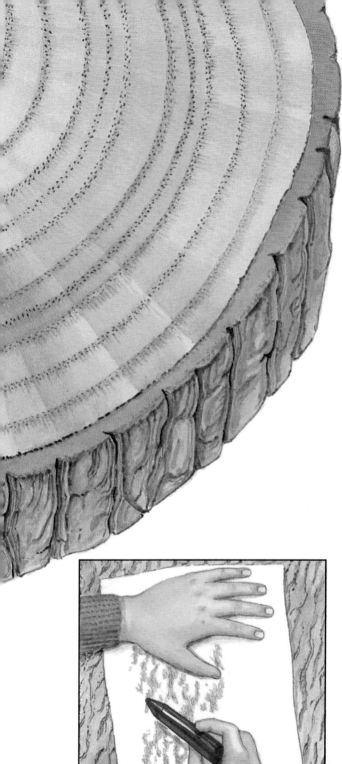

Counting Rings

If you find a tree stump or a pile of cut logs in a plantation, you can work out the age of the trees by counting the rings in the trunk. It is easiest to count the darker rings, showing the end of each year's growth. Measure the width of each ring to see how the amount of growth varies from year to year. If growing conditions are good, the rings will be wider and farther apart. Narrow rings show that growth has been slower in those years. Can you think of any reasons why?

Bark Rubbings

The bark of a tree protects it from damage, from drying out or from attack by insects. As the trunk grows, the bark grows, stretches and cracks like skin.

Lay a piece of paper against tree bark and rub over the top with a wax crayon. Don't rub too hard or you will tear the paper. How is the bark of each kind of tree different? How many different kinds of bark can you find? Can you identify trees just by looking at their bark?

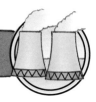

Plants often find it hard to grow because people have polluted the environment with poisonous waste products from homes, cars, factories, or farms.

How Polluted is the Air in your Area?

Make some sticky squares by gluing sticky-backed plastic on to cardboard. Fix them outside in different places. After a few days, look at them with a magnifying glass. How much dirt has each collected? Where are the most polluted places in your area? Where are plants growing best?

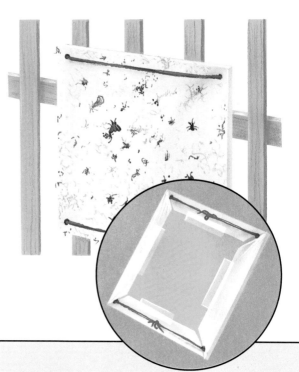

Looking for Lichens

Plants called lichens don't like pollution, such as acid rain. They have no roots and absorb any poisons in the air or water all over their surface. If the poisons build up, they may eventually kill the lichens. Small, flat lichens can cope with highish levels of pollution. So can crusty orange lichens, which grow mostly on stones. But leafy, bushy lichens can survive only in really clean air.

Go on a lichen hunt in your area. Look on walls, roofs, gravestones, and tree trunks. Which sort of lichens can you find? The type of lichen will give you a clue to the amount of pollution in your area. If the air is very polluted, you will not find any lichens at all.

▲ Acid rain is formed when poisonous gases from power plants, factories, and vehicle exhausts mix with water in the air. Acid rain damages plant growth and weakens the plant. Trees with needles are most likely to be affected.

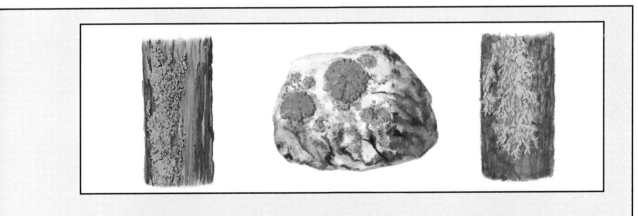

Medium pollution
Gray-green crusty lichens

Medium pollution
Orange crusty lichens

Clean air
Bushy, feathery lichens

TRUE OR FALSE?

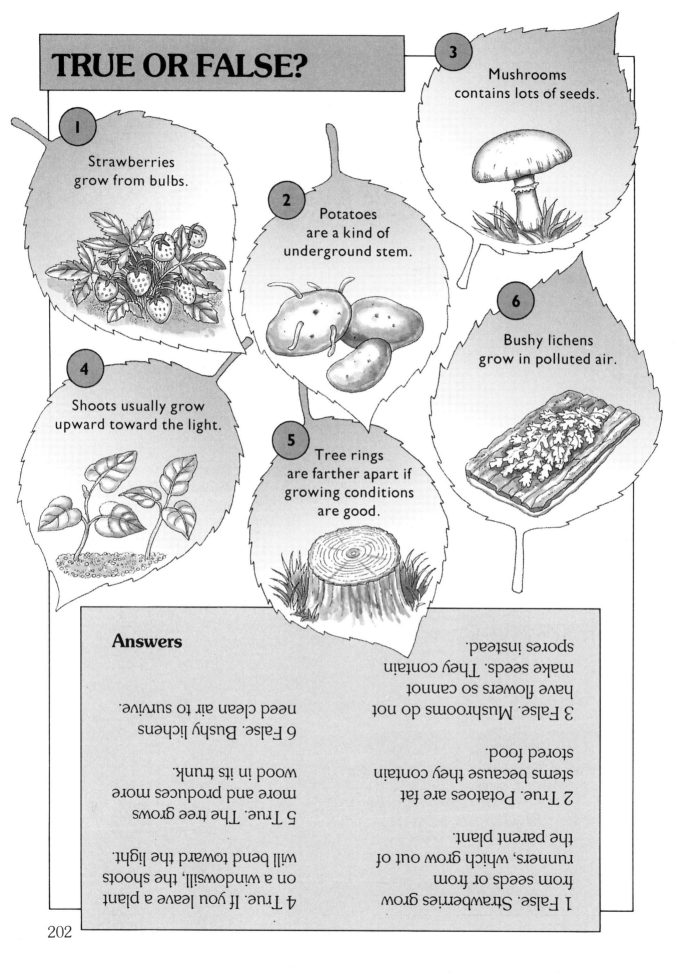

1. Strawberries grow from bulbs.

2. Potatoes are a kind of underground stem.

3. Mushrooms contains lots of seeds.

4. Shoots usually grow upward toward the light.

5. Tree rings are farther apart if growing conditions are good.

6. Bushy lichens grow in polluted air.

Answers

1 False. Strawberries grow from seeds or from runners, which grow out of the parent plant.

2 True. Potatoes are fat stems because they contain stored food.

3 False. Mushrooms do not have flowers so cannot make seeds. They contain spores instead.

4 True. If you leave a plant on a windowsill, the shoots will bend toward the light.

5 True. The tree grows more and produces more wood in its trunk.

6 False. Bushy lichens need clean air to survive.

Batteries and Magnets

What is inside a battery? Which materials let electricity pass through them? Why is a light bulb filament made of thin wire? Why are wires often covered in plastic? What are magnets made from? Which materials "stick" to magnets?

This section will help you to discover the answers to these questions and has lots of ideas for ways to investigate batteries and magnets.

BATTERIES AND MAGNETS

In this section, you can discover how to join batteries, bulbs, and wires into simple circuits, more about the pushing and pulling forces around magnets and some of the links between electricity and magnetism.

The section is divided into six different topics. Look out for the big headings with a circle at each end — like the one at the top of this page.

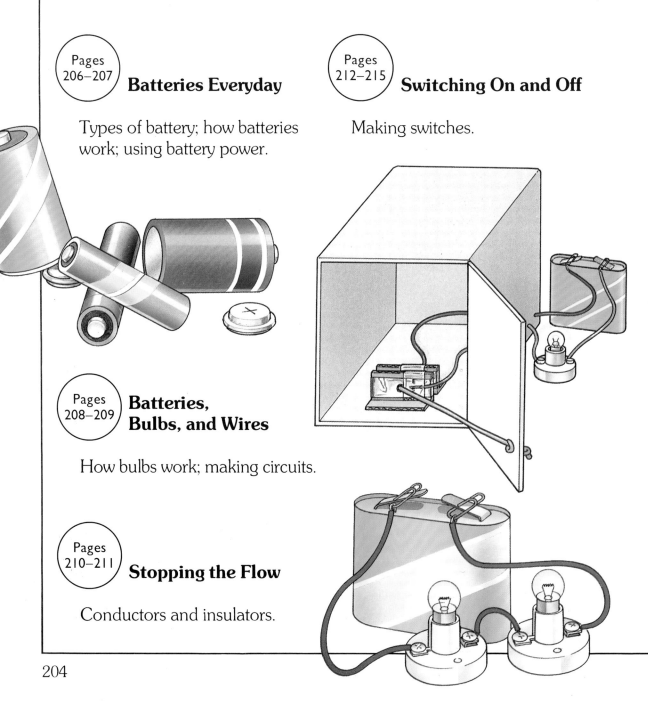

Pages 206–207

Batteries Everyday

Types of battery; how batteries work; using battery power.

Pages 212–215

Switching On and Off

Making switches.

Pages 208–209

Batteries, Bulbs, and Wires

How bulbs work; making circuits.

Pages 210–211

Stopping the Flow

Conductors and insulators.

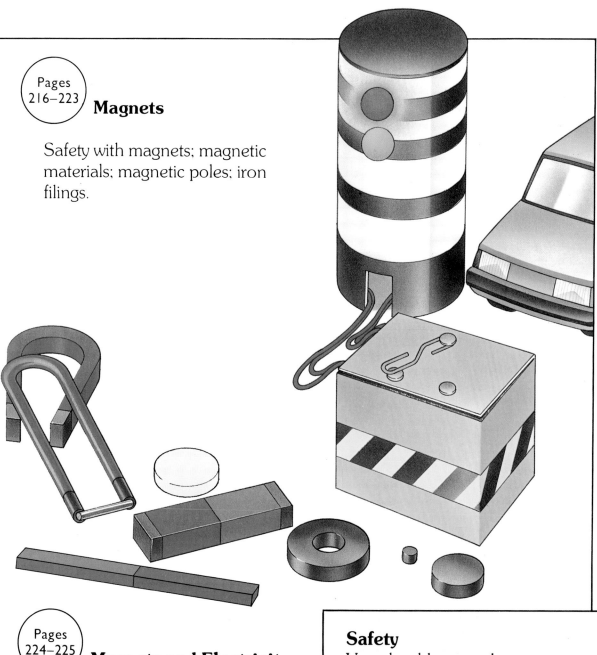
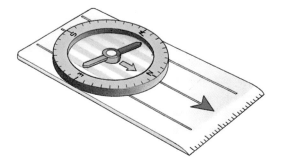
Safety

You should **never** do any experiments with the wires, plugs, or sockets in your home or school. The amount of electricity in these things makes them very dangerous. Electric shocks can kill you. Do not go near electricity pylons, overhead cables or substations. Electricity could jump across a gap and kill you.

Look carefully around your home, school, and in the stores and see how many different batteries you can find. What shapes and sizes are they? Small batteries are used inside watches, hearing aids, and pocket calculators. What other things can you think of that use battery power?

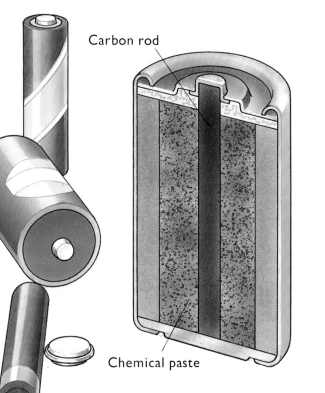

Carbon rod

Chemical paste

Batteries make and store electricity, which is a kind of energy. You cannot see electricity, but you can see that it makes things work. Electricity is made inside a battery by chemicals. Negative electrical charges collect in one part of a battery and positive electrical charges in another. This is shown by the plus and minus signs on a battery. You must **never** take a battery to pieces. The chemicals inside it are dangerous.

Batteries push electricity along wires, and their voltage is the pushing force of the battery. The voltage of batteries, usually printed on the sides, is much less than electricity from a plug or socket on the wall. So batteries are safer to use in investigations. They are also useful because they can be moved from place to place.

▲ How long do the batteries in your toys last before going "flat"? This happens when chemicals inside a battery are used up. When a battery is worn out, throw it away at once, as chemicals may leak out and cause damage. You should also take batteries out of things you are not going to use for a long time.

BATTERIES, BULBS, WIRES

To find out more about electricity, you can join up batteries, bulbs, and wires in lots of different ways. Here are some hints on how to do this.

Wires

Wires are made of metal, which carries electricity, with plastic coating on the outside. The plastic stops the electricity leaking out because it does not carry electricity. Before you use plastic-covered wire, strip a little plastic off the ends.

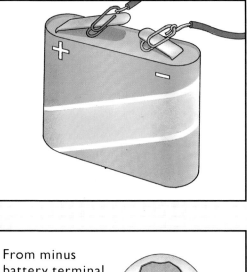

Solid core

Stranded

Twin cable

Batteries

4.5 volt batteries are the most useful for your investigations. It is easier to join wires to batteries with flat ends. The ends of a battery are called terminals. You can use paper clips, crocodile clips or tape to join wires to battery terminals.

Bulbs

You will need several small, screw-in bulbs — the kind used in flashlights or bicycle lamps. Use a 2.5 volt or a 3.5 volt bulb with a 4.5 volt battery. Use a 6 volt bulb with a 9 volt battery. You need to touch one wire to the bottom of the bulb and the other wire to the side of the casing.

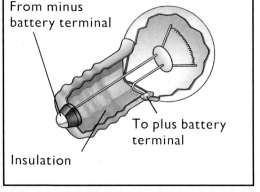

From minus battery terminal

To plus battery terminal

Insulation

► A light bulb is a hollow glass shape full of special gas. The glass is attached to a metal tube with wires inside. Electricity flows into the bulb, up one wire, across a coiled wire called a filament, down the other wire and out of the bulb. The filament is made of very thin wire so it is hard for electricity to squeeze through. The way that wire holds back the electricity is called resistance. This makes the filament so hot that it glows and so gives off light.

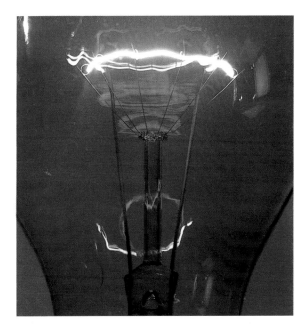

Bulb Holders

When you are doing investigations, it is hard to hold the wires, batteries and bulbs. It helps to fix the bulbs into bulb holders. You can buy these or make some yourself. The pictures show you how to fix the bulb in place.

If you buy one, look at it carefully to see how screws on the side connect up with the two connections on the bulb. To attach the wires to the bulb holder, use a screwdriver to loosen the screws on the sides and fix the wires underneath.

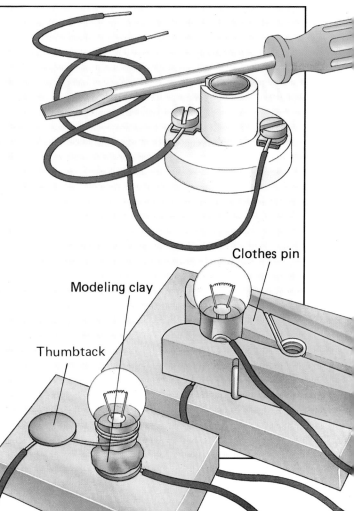

Clothes pin

Modeling clay

Thumbtack

STOPPING THE FLOW

Which materials does electricity flow through? Make a collection of materials to test, such as paper, metal objects (keys, forks, and coins), cloth, plastic, a stone, a rubber, cork, and wood.

Make a circuit with a battery, a bulb, and two wires. Leave the ends of the wires free. Use each object in turn to complete the circuit. Does the bulb light up? Sometimes the paint on objects stops the electricity flowing through. Scratch a little paint off the surface to see if it makes any difference.

▶ The insulators used in power plants or on electricity pylons are made of ceramic materials, such as porcelain. They have an important job to do because the electricity here is at a very high voltage and is extremely dangerous. **Never** go near electricity pylons, substations or power stations. **Electricity can kill you.**

Sort your collection into two groups — materials that let electricity pass through and materials that do not let electricity pass through.

Materials that let electricity pass through them easily are called good conductors. Metals are good conductors, which is why wires are made of metal. Bad conductors are often called insulators. Rubber and plastic are good insulators. Wires are often covered in rubber or plastic. The insulators keep the electricity in the wire and stop it leaking out, so it is less dangerous.

Spoon and Fork Circuit

Can you make a circuit using a spoon and fork to conduct the electricity instead of wires? You will probably need to tape the bulb to the battery to hold it in place.

Tape bulb to battery

Spoon upside down for good connection

We use good conductors to make switches. When a switch is off, there is a gap in a circuit so electricity cannot flow. When a switch is on, the gap is closed up to complete the circuit. Electricity can flow right around the circuit to make something work.

Switches are very useful in investigations with batteries, bulbs, and wires. Here are some ideas for different ways to make switches:

Paper Clip

Use a paper clip to link two thumbtacks. When you move the clip away from one tack, you break the circuit and turn the switch off. You could use cardboard wrapped in foil instead of a paper clip.

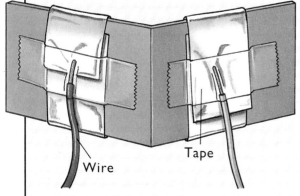

Wire

Tape

Folded Cardboard

Wrap foil around the ends of a piece of folded cardboard. When the folded cardboard presses the two pieces of foil together, it completes the circuit and turns the switch on. This is a kind of pressure switch.

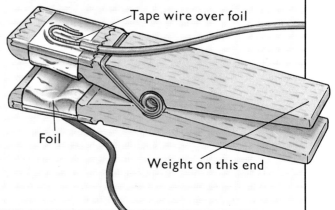

Tape wire over foil

Foil

Weight on this end

Clothes Pin

Wrap the ends of a clothes pin in foil. A weight pressing on the other end turns the switch off. If the weight is taken away, the foil ends spring together and turn the switch on.

Make a Burglar Alarm

You will need:
A large box to make a "safe", a battery, a bulb or buzzer, cardboard, foil, scissors, tape, string, wire or thread, colored pencils, treasure for your "safe".

1. Cut two pieces of cardboard and wrap them in foil.
2. Fix one wire to each piece of cardboard with tape.
3. Cut two small holes in the side of the box and push the wires through from the inside.
4. Make a circuit outside the box with the battery, the wires, and the bulb.
5. Use string or wire to join both pieces of cardboard to the door, as in the picture. Arrange the pieces of cardboard in the "safe," so that they are not touching.
6. Decorate your "safe," put some treasure inside and close the door.

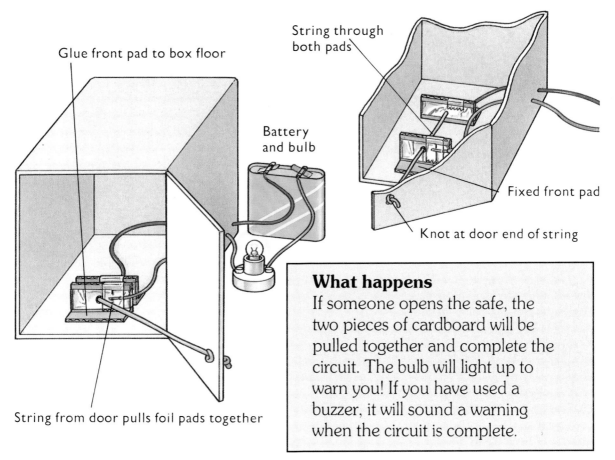

Glue front pad to box floor

String through both pads

Battery and bulb

Fixed front pad

Knot at door end of string

String from door pulls foil pads together

What happens
If someone opens the safe, the two pieces of cardboard will be pulled together and complete the circuit. The bulb will light up to warn you! If you have used a buzzer, it will sound a warning when the circuit is complete.

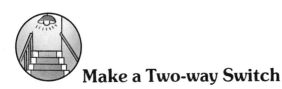

Make a Two-way Switch

Do you know of a light that can be switched on or off from different places? This needs a special kind of switch called a two-way switch.

You will need to make two switches (see page 212) and wire them into a circuit like the one in the picture.

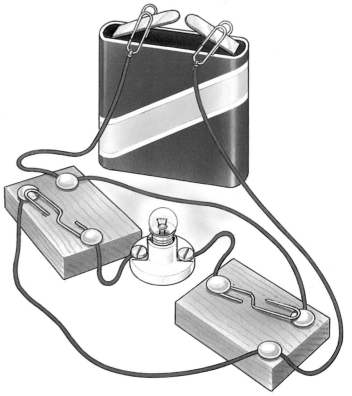

You should find that the bulb can be turned on or off using either one of the switches to break a circuit or complete a circuit. In a building, much longer wires connect the two switches together in a similar way.

Make a Dimmer Switch

You will need:
a battery, a bulb, two pieces of plastic-covered wire, a piece of bare wire, a pencil.

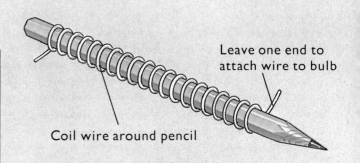

Leave one end to attach wire to bulb

Coil wire around pencil

1. Coil the bare wire round and round the pencil.
2. Make a circuit with the battery, bulb, and plastic-covered wires.
3. Twist the end of one of the plastic-covered wires around the end of the coiled wire.
4. Touch the end of the other plastic-covered wire to the coiled wire at different points. Does the brightness of the bulb change?

▲ Resistors, such as the ones on this circuit board, change the flow of electricity. They are used in light dimmer switches and volume controls.

What happens

When a lot of the coiled wire is in the circuit, the electricity has to push hard through the wire. There is a lot of resistance, so the bulb is dim. If a shorter length of coil is in the circuit, there is less resistance to the electricity. More energy is left to light the bulb, so it glows more brightly.

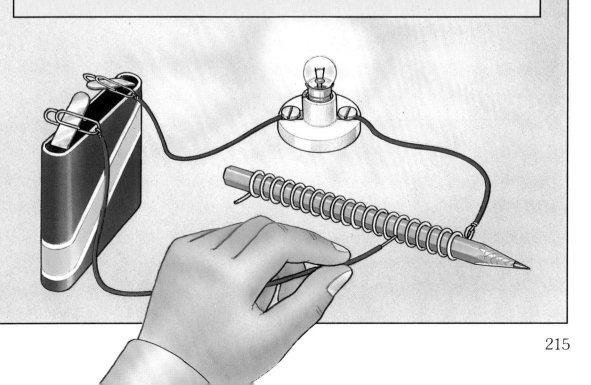

MAGNETS

Have you got a magnet? What shape is it? Magnets come in all sorts of shapes and sizes, from long, thin ones to the round ones on refrigerator magnets. See how many shapes and sizes you can find.

Magnets are very useful for sticking things together without using glue. They are used to keep the doors of refrigerators shut. They are also used to hold the pieces on the board in travel games. Can you find any other uses for magnets?

Safety with Magnets

Magnets can damage watches, televisions, computer discs, videos, and tape recorders. Make sure you keep magnets well away from these things.

▶ The first magnets were made more than 2,000 years ago from lodestone, a special black stone which pulls iron materials toward it. It contains an iron ore called magnetite. Nowadays, most magnets are made from iron or steel.

Magnetic Materials

Magnets have the power to pull
some materials, called magnetic
materials, toward them. To see
what is magnetic, collect objects
made from different materials,
such as paper, wood, metal,
plastic, glass, and rubber.

Which objects "stick" to your magnet? Can you feel the pull of the
magnet through your fingers?

Sort your collection into magnetic materials and non-magnetic
materials. To keep a record of your results, you could draw a chart.

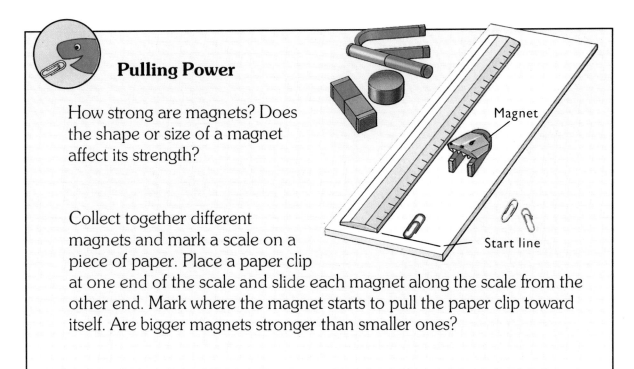

Pulling Power

How strong are magnets? Does
the shape or size of a magnet
affect its strength?

Collect together different
magnets and mark a scale on a
piece of paper. Place a paper clip
at one end of the scale and slide each magnet along the scale from the
other end. Mark where the magnet starts to pull the paper clip toward
itself. Are bigger magnets stronger than smaller ones?

Magnet

Start line

Stopping the Power

Can some materials block the pulling power of a magnet? See if your magnet still works through glass, paper, or wood.

Plastic

Wood

Card

Drop a paper clip into a bowl of water. Can you use a magnet to pick up the paper clip without getting your fingers wet?

Magnetic Maze

1. Draw a maze on one side of a paper plate.
2. Ask a friend to hold the plate for you.
3. Put a paper clip at the start of the maze and hold a bar magnet under the plate.
4. Time how long it takes to pull the paper clip through the maze without touching any of the lines. Have a race with your friend. Who has the steadiest hand?

Maze on plate

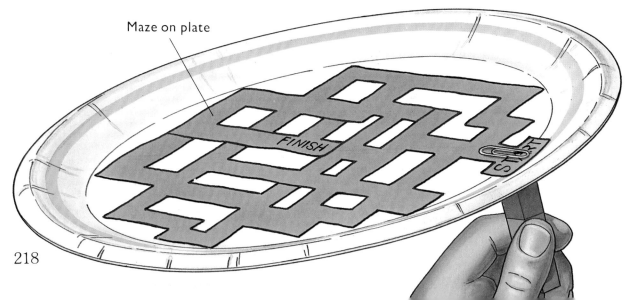

FINISH

START

Cut out front of box to make curtains

Characters

Stick

Paperclip

Magnet

Magnetic Theater

You will need:

thick cardboard, thin card, scissors, paint or crayons, tape, glue, thin sticks, a cardboard box, small magnets.

1. Draw and cut out a model theater stage from thick cardboard. Color the scenery and curtains with the paints or crayons.
2. Cut away the top of the box. Turn the box on its side and glue the stage to the bottom and side. Leave about 2 inches space under the stage. Cut away the bottom of the box below the level of the stage. Stick it at the front to hide the gap.
3. Draw and color in your actors on thin card. Cut them out, with a piece of card at the bottom. Bend this back so they stand up.
4. Tape a paper clip on the bent card behind each actor.
5. Tape a magnet to each of the thin sticks.
6. Put the actors on stage. Slide the magnetic sticks in through the cut bottom of the box, so they are under the stage. Move the actors with the magnets.

 ## Pull and Push

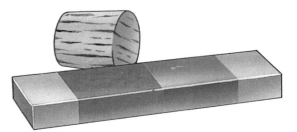

The pulling force of a magnet is strongest at certain points, called the poles of the magnet. In a long, straight bar magnet, the poles are at either end of the magnet. They are called the North and South Poles. The poles of one magnet do not always pull the poles of other magnets toward them. Sometimes they push them away. This investigation will show you more about how magnets behave.

Magnetic Dolphins

1. Draw two dolphin shapes on cardboard. Cut them out.
2. Glue or tape bar magnets to two corks and stick a dolphin on top of each cork and magnet.
3. Float the dolphins in a bowl of water. What happens when you push the dolphins together?
4. Turn one of the dolphins around. What happens?

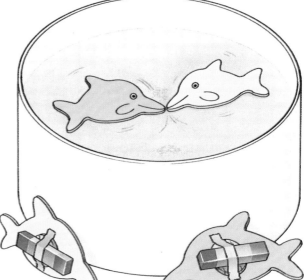

What happens
The dolphins stick together if the magnets are one way round. But when you turn one magnet around, it will push the other dolphin away. Two North Poles or two South Poles will push each other apart, but a North Pole and a South Pole will stick together. Magnets will stick together if the poles are different, and will push each other apart if the poles are the same.

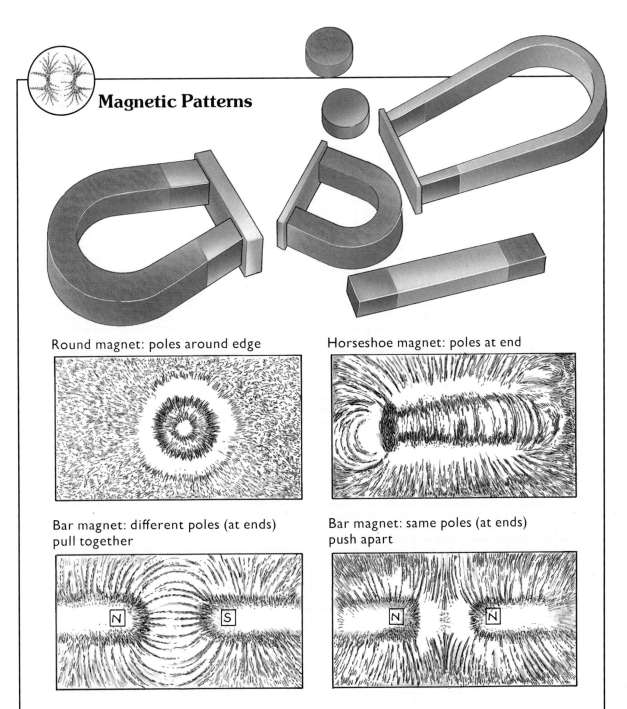

Magnetic Patterns

Round magnet: poles around edge

Horseshoe magnet: poles at end

Bar magnet: different poles (at ends)
pull together

Bar magnet: same poles (at ends)
push apart

We cannot usually see the pushing and pulling forces around a magnet.
But by scattering some iron filings on a piece of paper and placing a
magnet under the paper, some of the lines of force become clear.
Where the magnet gives out a strong force, lots of iron filings group
together. Where the force is weaker, the filings are farther apart.

With two poles that are the same, the filings show that the poles are
pushing apart. With two poles that are different, the filings show how
the poles pull together.

Pointing North and South

If you hang a magnet up by a thread or float it on water, it spins slowly. When it comes to rest, it points toward the North and South Poles of the Earth. (This is why magnets are said to have North and South Poles.) The Earth itself has magnetic powers and is like a giant magnet. The Earth's huge magnetic force pushes and pulls smaller magnets. Did you know that a compass needle is a magnet?

To find out more about magnets, make one yourself.

Make a Compass

> **You will need:**
> a magnet, a needle, a piece of cork or polystyrene, a bowl of water, a compass.

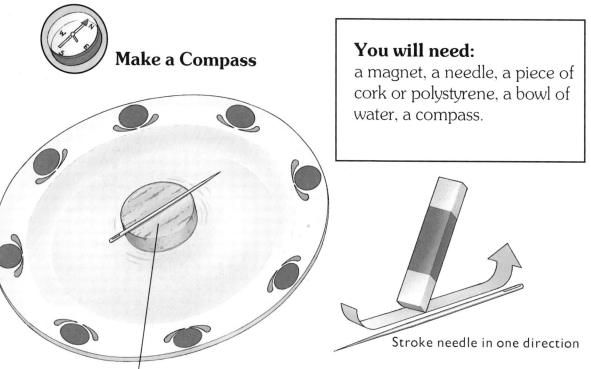

Cork with needle on top

Stroke needle in one direction

1. Stroke the end of the magnet along the needle about 50 times. Stroke it in the same direction each time and hold the needle away after each stroke. This will turn the needle into a magnet.
2. Put the needle on top of the cork or polystyrene and float it in the bowl of water.
3. Place a compass next to the bowl of water and check that your needle points in the same direction as the compass needle.

▲ Lodestone (meaning "the stone that leads") was used to guide people centuries ago. Nowadays, magnetic compass needles are used on ships and airplanes as well as on land to help people find their way.

Did you know that you can make magnets with electricity? When electricity flows along a wire, it makes the wire magnetic. You can test this by building a circuit with a switch. Put a compass near the wire and watch to see what happens to the compass needle when you switch on the electricity.

What happens
The magnetic force in the wire will push and pull the magnetic compass needle and make it swing about.

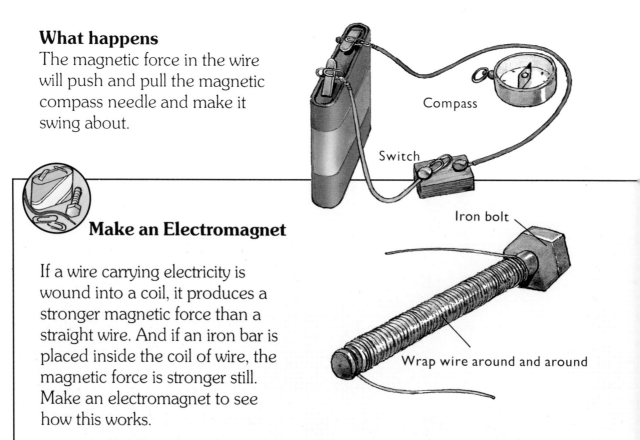

Compass

Switch

Iron bolt

Wrap wire around and around

Make an Electromagnet

If a wire carrying electricity is wound into a coil, it produces a stronger magnetic force than a straight wire. And if an iron bar is placed inside the coil of wire, the magnetic force is stronger still. Make an electromagnet to see how this works.

1. Wind the long piece of wire around the bolt, keeping the coils close together. The more times you wind the wire around the bolt, the stronger the magnet.
2. Join one end of the wire to a battery terminal and the other end of the wire to the switch.

You will need:
a large iron bolt, a nail, a few feet of insulated wire, a short piece of wire, a switch, a battery, paper clips, a matchbox, a wooden frame, thread.

▲ This electromagnet is sorting scrap metals from other non-magnetic materials. Electromagnets are useful because they only work when electricity is switched on.

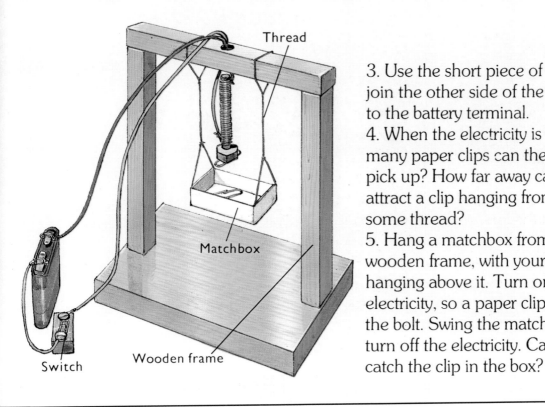

Thread

Matchbox

Wooden frame

Switch

3. Use the short piece of wire to join the other side of the switch to the battery terminal.

4. When the electricity is on, how many paper clips can the bolt pick up? How far away can it attract a clip hanging from some thread?

5. Hang a matchbox from a wooden frame, with your bolt hanging above it. Turn on the electricity, so a paper clip sticks to the bolt. Swing the matchbox and turn off the electricity. Can you catch the clip in the box?

GLOSSARY

Acid A sour substance which is the chemical opposite of an **alkali**. It contains hydrogen and can be replaced by metals.

Acid rain Rain that is more acidic than normal because it has chemicals from vehicle exhausts, power plants, and factories dissolved in it.

Aileron Flaps on the wings of an airplane that can be moved up and down to make the plane turn left or right.

Airfoil A wing that is curved on top and flat underneath.

Air presssure The effect caused by the **weight** of all the air in the **atmosphere** pressing down on everything on Earth. Low air pressure usually brings bad weather and high air pressure usually brings good weather.

Alkali The chemical opposite of an **acid**. An alkali neutralizes an acid to produce a salt and water.

Atmosphere The layer of invisible gases around the Earth. It is made up mainly of **oxygen** and nitrogen.

Axle The rod on which a wheel turns.

Ball bearings Small steel balls used to reduce friction and help parts of machines move more easily.

Barometer An instrument for measuring **air pressure.**

Bulb A short underground stem wrapped in swollen, fleshy leaf bases.

Center of gravity The place where the weight of an object seems to be concentrated. It is sometimes called the balancing point.

Circuit A pathway for electricity. A circuit has to be complete for electricity to flow. A switch is a break or a gap in a circuit.

Compressed air Air that has been squashed or compressed into a small space.

Conductor A material such as copper which allows electricity to flow through it easily.

Convection The transfer of heat in a liquid or gas by the movement of the liquid or the gas itself.

Decibel (dB) A unit used to measure the loudness of sound. Conversation is about 60 decibels and the sound of a jet engine is about 120 decibels.

Density The mass or "weight" of a substance per unit of volume. In other words, how heavy something is for its size.

Displacement The amount of water or other liquid pushed out of the way by a floating object. If an object weighs the same as the liquid it displaces, it will float. If the object weighs more than the maximum amount of water it can displace, it will sink.

Drag The **resistance** to movement in water or air.

Dyes Chemical substances used to color cloth and other materials.

Eclipse An eclipse of the Sun (Solar eclipse) occurs when the Moon stops sunlight from reaching the Earth. An eclipse of the Moon (Lunar eclipse) occurs when the Earth stops sunlight from reaching the Moon.

Elastic material A material that stretches, but goes back to its original shape after the stretching force is removed.

Electromagnet An iron rod with coils of wire wrapped around it. When an electric current is passed through the wire, the rod becomes magnetic.

Elevators Flaps on the tail of an airplane which can be moved to make the plane climb or dive.

Filter A screen that stops things, such as colored light, from passing through it.

Force A push or a pull that makes an object change its speed, direction or shape.

Friction A force that occurs when two surfaces rub against each other. It tends to slow things down or to stop them moving, and it produces heat.

Fulcrum The point at which a lever pivots or turns.

Gear wheels Wheels with teeth around the edge which fit together. Such wheels can act to change the speed or direction of movement.

Germination The moment when a **seed** starts to grow its first shoot, roots and leaves. For germination to take place, the seed needs the right amount of warmth, moisture and **oxygen**.

Girdle scar A series of rings or cicles on a twig marking the spot where the bud scales have fallen off. It shows where the twig starts to grow each year.

Gravity The force of attraction between any two objects that have mass. (Mass is the amount of matter a body contains.) Gravity pulls everything on Earth down to the ground and gives things their **weight**.

Hurricane A very violent storm that forms over the west Atlantic Ocean. It is called a typhoon in the Far East and a cyclone in Australia.

Hydrometer An instrument for measuring the density of liquids.

Insulator A material such as plastic that does not let electricity flow through it easily.

Kaleidoscope A tube through which patterns of symmetrical reflections can be seen.

Lever A bar or pole that swings or pivots on a fixed point called a **fulcrum.**

Lift The force pressing up against flying or gliding things to keep them up in the air.

Liquid A runny substance which has no shape. It takes on the shape of the container it is in.

Lodestone A type of rock which is a natural magnet. It contains an iron ore called magnetite.

Magnetic poles The places on a magnet where the magnetic pull is strongest.

Maracas Club-like percussion instruments filled with beans. They are played by shaking.

Magnetism The invisible pulling force of a magnet on things made of iron or steel.

Materials The substances from which things are made.

Megaphone A large trumpet-shaped instrument for carrying the sound of a voice over a distance.

Mirror A smooth, shiny surface that produces good reflections.

Mordant Substance used to "fix" coloring material on another substance, so that the colors will not run.

Opaque Something that does not allow light to pass through it. You cannot *see* through opaque material.

Oxygen An invisible gas with no taste or smell which all living things need to stay alive. Oxygen is also needed for things to burn.

Percussion instruments Musical instruments played by striking, shaking or scraping. They include drums, xylophones, guiro, and maracas.

Periscope An instrument which uses the light reflected between mirrors in a tube to allow people to see things otherwise out of sight.

Pigment A substance which gives anything its color.

Pollution The spoiling and poisoning of the environment with harmful substances.

Pulley A wheel with a groove around the edge for carrying a rope or a cable. It is used to help people lift heavy weights.

Primary color One of three colors which mix together to produce any other color. The primary colors of paint are red, yellow, and blue. The primary colors of light are red, green, and blue.

Reed A separate device fixed inside a woodwind instrument which makes the air vibrate to produce the sound. Clarinets and saxophones have one reed; all other woodwind instruments, such as oboes, have two reeds.

Reflection The way in which rays of light bounce back from a surface.

Resistance The opposition to the flow of an electric current which is measured in ohms. The more resistance a wire has, the less current it carries.

Resonance When the vibrations of a substance, such as the wood of a violin, match the vibrations of the air which produce the sound.

Runner A long, thin stem which grows out from a plant. New plants grow at intervals along the runner.

Screw A slope wrapped in a spiral around a central rod. It changes a turning

228

force into a much greater straight line force.

Seed A reproductive structure consisting of a young plant and a food store wrapped in a protective coat. It is produced by flowering plants and plants with cones. In the right conditions, a seed will grow into a new plant.

Shadow A dark area which forms behind an object when it blocks out a source of light. Shadows are places where light does not shine.

Sound box A hollow box with an opening which is placed behind something producing a sound to make the sound louder.

Speed of sound Sound travels faster through solids or liquids than it does through air. The speed of sound in air is about 1,080 feet per second. The speed of sound through water is about 4,690 feet per second.

Streamlined Something with a smooth, slim shape which cuts through air or water easily.

Stringed instruments Musical instruments which produce sounds by vibrating strings. They include guitars, violins, and sitars.

Surface tension The pulling force that holds

together the surface of liquids such as water and makes them appear to have a thin elastic "skin."

Symmetrical object An object that can be divided into two or more parts which are exactly the same.

Translucent Something that lets some light through but scatters it. If you look through a translucent material, things look blurred.

Transparent Something that lets light go straight through it. You can see clearly through transparent materials.

Tuber A rounded swelling at the end of an underground root or shoot which contains stored food. A potato is a tuber.

Vibration When something moves to and fro. Sounds are caused by the air vibrating very fast, causing changes in the pressure of the air.

Voltage The force which pushes electricity along wires. The higher the voltage, the bigger the electric current.

Wedge Two slopes stuck back to back which can be pushed into a gap to force two objects apart.

Weight The force exerted on objects by the pull of **gravity**. Things have weight because gravity pulls them to the ground.

INDEX

Acknowledgments

The publishers wish to thank the following
artists for contributing to this book:

Peter Bull
Peter Dennis (Linda Rogers Associates)
Kuo Kang Chen
Eleanor Ludgate of Jillian Burgess Illustrations
Josephine Martin of Garden Studio
Patricia Newell of John Martin & Artists Ltd
John Scorey

The publishers also wish to thank the following
for kindly supplying photographs for this book:

Heather Angel/Biofotos
JW Automarine
Biofotos
Boeing
Ron Boardman
J Allan Cash
Dylon
Mark Edwards/Still Pictures
A.G.E FotoStock
French Government Tourist Office
The Guardian
Michal Holford
Lesley Howling
Chris Howes
Hutchinson Library
IMITOR
Frank Lane Picture Agency
Life Agency
Pat Morris
NASA
National Grid Company
Nature Photographers
NHPA/Stephen Dalton
NHPA/Silvestris
NHPA/David Woodfall
NTN Bearings
Picturepoint
Jane Placca
Premier Percussion
Quadrant
Royal Albert Hall
Science Museum, London
Science Photo Library
Spectrum
Supersport Photos
Thames Water plc
Tim Woodstock
Zefa